# Sussex
## Walks

# Sussex
# Walks

Written by **Deirdre Huston**

 Copyright © 2013 Vertebrate Graphics Ltd and Deirdre Huston

Published by Vertebrate Publishing

ISBN 978-1-906148-68-3

Front cover photo: Chalk path near Wilmington, **Route 11**.
Back cover photos: *Top left:* East Head Shingle Spit, **Route 20**. *Top right:* Broadstone Heath, **Route 1**. *Bottom left:* Pair of common blue butterflies  Photo: Kieron Huston.

Photography by Deirdre Huston, unless otherwise credited.

 All maps reproduced by permission of Ordnance Survey on behalf of The Controller of Her Majesty's Stationery Office. © Crown Copyright. 100025218

 Design and production by Jane Beagley. www.v-graphics.co.uk

# Contents

Ashdown Forest

# Acknowledgements

**One of the most enjoyable aspects of researching this guidebook was exploring new terrain with friends and family – an excuse for more brilliant days out walking in good company.**

Many thanks to Bev Angel, Olive and Robin Huston, Pat and Bob Rayland, and my ever-loving mainstays, Ian, Sean, Tegan and Rory who know only too well that each book represents a whole new journey.

I would like to offer sincere thanks to my efficient and diverse group of route-testers who not only helped make the book more accurate but gently reminded me of the varied elements which they value such as history, good pubs, literary links, particular landscapes, environmental information and great views. A special mention must go to Gösta Luthman, who tested a wide variety of walks in all sorts of conditions, providing detailed yet encouraging feedback. I am hoping that in return he has developed a love of walking!

Other route-testers include Susanne Waldschmidt, who has completed all 18 National Trails in the UK. She is an active member of Long Distance Walkers Association. Writing pal, Alan Woodruff provided a great sounding board for ideas and tested several walks with his friend, Tony Donovan. Old friend, Carol Turner, helped out too in the Ashdown Forest. Thanks also to Mandy and Stuart Dale who took time on their day off together to help out and who also tested a route with their children, Dominique and Matt. All your feedback was invaluable and much appreciated.

Thanks to you all for becoming involved in the project and stepping forward when needed.

# Introduction

Walking is a simple pleasure which offers many rewards. This guidebook aims to help you enjoy walking on several levels. This is more than a country walks book.

Firstly, the nitty-gritty. This guidebook offers 20 walks through varied and interesting landscapes such as open downland, valuable chalk grassland and canal and river wetlands; across rare chalk heath and heather and gorse-clad heathland, through broadleaf and coniferous forest and along evolving coastline and eroding chalk cliffs. Explore the South Downs National Park, meander through the agricultural Low and High Weald and amble along ridge tops in the Ashdown Forest. My aim is that even novice walkers heading off alone can feel confident about setting out to explore pastures new. Trails have been tested by a dedicated group of walkers, ranging from beginners to the very experienced, from families to fanatics. Most of the walks are between three and seven miles with a couple of longer ones for those who want more.

Routes often include characterful country pubs; the kinds of places which might stock local food or cook simple fare freshly. In short, the type of pub we'd be happy to discover ourselves. Stop for a picnic and the walk will cost you little more than the energy it takes to step forward. In return, a walk outdoors keeps you healthy, recharges your batteries physically and mentally, offering the chance to laugh, relax and enjoy the world around us.

Take a moment here or there to pause and enjoy where you are. Hear the astonishing song of a skylark overhead; look down and notice the unusual pink of a downland flower or the strangeness of fungi; breathe in and see if you can taste salt air on the sea breeze. Feel the soft breeze on your skin when you stand on top of the downs or the flint path underfoot on a downland descent. Small moments are significant in enhancing our experience of the world and when we interact with our environment, it makes us curious. We react by wanting to know more.

So secondly, I've carefully chosen landscapes to spark your interest and designed trails to encourage you to delve that little bit deeper. What makes the landscape special? Why is it a nature reserve or a Site of Special Scientific Interest? What are the different types of habitat and what is being done to help preserve these vital ecosystems? I have included information to answer such questions concisely so that you can enjoy your walk in a wider context.

On a third level, this book offers you the chance to be creative. A deep human reaction to our natural environment is to create. As a teacher of photography and creative writing, this process interests me and I know interests many of you too. Many writers and artists find inspiration in places. They draw on their observations of locations to create fictional settings or poetic phrases. I've included routes which include places of literary significance such as Pooh Bridge (Christopher Robin and Winnie) and Charleston (the Bloomsbury Set) so that you can yourself explore places which have inspired writers.

But why stop there? Why not be creative yourself? Share in this process. Take your camera or notebook along and see which tiny detail or huge vista inspires you. Each route offers you a creative starting point for a photographic and/or writing task, a theme to develop your ideas, words or images around. Use the starting point as a spur to your creativity and enjoy this opportunity to be creative outdoors in the ever-changing light of the natural landscape.

So here they are. Twenty walks for you to enjoy.

Deirdre

# How to Use the Creative Starting Points

The creative starting points are designed to be fun and stimulating – a light-hearted way to add enjoyment to your walk. Readers who are more serious about their creative medium, (maybe writing, photography or something entirely different), may find them useful and interesting mechanisms for kick-starting ideas and developing their work. Any creative process encourages observation and reflection. Take the chance to see places through your own eyes, capture your own unique image, describe a place the way you see it.

The starting point may mean different things to different people. Each individual brings their own personality, experience and interests to a theme. As soon as you read the starting point, your brain will start ticking over, perhaps without you even being aware of it. The physical action of walking can be good for enabling thoughts to process. Be open to what comes to mind; let your thoughts bubble to the surface. Don't worry if the emerging ideas and the things you notice aren't what you are expecting or perhaps hoping for. Sometimes there's nothing wrong with the obvious and sometimes it pays to look behind the scenes or to examine the tiniest of details.

There are a cross-section of starting points across the book. Some are one word, others a pair of contrasting or associated ideas. You don't have to use them all – simply select those that appeal. Sometimes it's worth choosing the ideas that you're less keen on in order to challenge yourself. I have chosen them with an awareness of the landscape through which you will walk. Each of these trails is unique and they'll be different each time you walk them, depending on season, time of day, changing light and weather. Actively engage with your environment, using all your senses. If something catches your attention, stop and try to work out what it is. It may not be an external noise or sight but an internal emotion, a feeling about something, that you want to capture. Look for the emotional triggers in the sensory landscape through which you walk. You may choose to mix and match starting points between walks. Feel free to experiment.

### Writing

There isn't space in this book to provide ideas for specific writing structures or genres. Take the starting point and make it into whatever you wish. You may simply list words. Words may turn to phrases. Try not to question or judge your efforts but let the words evolve. You may find that they start to shape a poem or a piece of prose – maybe a dialogue or a description. You may find that you imagine a visual scene from a story or a page from a book. Make notes, write 'sketches' to enable you to explore the idea at a later date or stop and write in detail whilst in the setting.

### Photography

You might limit your images to the theme or use it to kick-start a wider approach. Are you capturing a spontaneous scene or planning the image by anticipating, for example, the movement of a distant silhouette? Your image may tell a story or it may be an abstract study of colour or pattern. Sometimes, in this digital era, it pays to focus on why we are taking an image, what exactly we want to capture and how we can make a place our own. Take lots of images or restrict yourself to ten careful shots. The choice is yours.

Don't worry if you're not immediately inspired or if you hit a blank. Enjoy the walk – inspiration doesn't arrive to order! We all love that creative 'rush' when it happens and sometimes, it's worth the wait.

# 'We wunt be druv' *(Unofficial Sussex motto – 'We won't be driven')*

## How to Use this Book

Discover how the ancient kingdom of Sussex has evolved as you follow our trails through ancient forest and rare heathland, along rivers and up downland escarpments; across wealden fields, down chalk bostals and through marshy carr. We cannot promise to take you everywhere in this large county but we can give you glimpses of much that it offers. Walk in the footsteps of Roman soldiers, gaze into iron-industry hammer ponds and race sticks under Pooh Bridge. See how Sussex farming is developing today and observe for yourself why some areas are significant enough to require protection as nature reserves or Sites of Special Scientific Interest.

This book should provide you with all the information that you need for an enjoyable, trouble-free and successful walk. The following tips should help.

We strongly recommend that you invest in the maps listed on page xiii. They are essential even if you are familiar with the area – you may need to cut short the walk or take an alternative route.

Choose your route. Consider the time you have available and the abilities/level of experience of all members of your party.

We recommend that you study the route description carefully before setting off. Cross-reference this to your map so that you've got a good sense of general orientation in case you need an escape route. Make sure that you are familiar with the symbols used on the maps.

No more delays. Time to get walking!

### Walking Speed

Most of the walks described here are between about three and eight miles in length. Two to three miles an hour is a relaxed walking speed for many people but will depend on terrain, ascent, fitness and how often you stop to look around.

**Ascent:** The total amount of climbing throughout the whole walk. It's a useful guide to how strenuous a walk might be.

## Navigation

For most walks in this guide, following the route description in combination with the route map provided should be sufficient. However it is recommended you carry with you the appropriate Ordnance Survey Explorer series map as a back up. These are shown for each walk. Sussex is covered by seven maps in the 1:25,000 series:

- Ordnance Survey Explorer 120: Chichester
- Ordnance Survey Explorer 121: Arundel and Pulborough
- Ordnance Survey Explorer 122: Brighton and Hove
- Ordnance Survey Explorer 123: Eastbourne and Beachy Head
- Ordnance Survey Explorer 124: Hastings and Bexhill
- Ordnance Survey Explorer 134: Crawley and Horsham
- Ordnance Survey Explorer 135: Ashdown Forest

### Footpaths and Rights of Way

All the walks in this guide follow public rights of way or other routes with public access, including '*permitted*' or '*concession*' footpaths.

## Safety

It is strongly advised that appropriate footwear be worn – walking boots designed to provide stability and security on uneven and slippery terrain. Chalk paths are notoriously slippery! A waterproof, windproof jacket is essential and waterproof legwear is strongly recommended. Sufficient insulated clothing should also be worn or carried, appropriate to the type of walk planned and the time of year. Keep an eye on the weather forecast and carry waterproofs and extra layers or sunblock and a hat. Carry lots of food and drink, including an emergency supply. It's surprising how quickly you can become depleted and/or dehydrated, especially at the end of the day. Stay away from cliff edges. Cliff erosion is not always obvious and can be fatal. Take extra precautions if walking alone and always tell somebody where you are going, giving a rough outline of the route if possible. Anybody can have an unexpected fall.

Take a mobile phone but don't rely on it – coverage can be patchy, especially on the Downs, and batteries go flat!

### Mountain Rescue

In case of accident or similar requiring mountain rescue assistance, **dial 999** and ask for **POLICE – MOUNTAIN RESCUE**. Be prepared to give a 6-figure grid reference of you position.

### Food and Drink

Always carry water. Dark chocolate, dried fruit and nuts are all good for an energy boost. If you're planning to visit a pub, contact them first. It's all too common to arrive in a village and discover that the pub's closed down. Cafes and kiosks may keep odd hours too. We can't include these details because things change but we can flag up pubs that we'd be happy to arrive at. There's something very satisfying about 'discovering' a country pub mid-walk and stopping for sustenance.

## The Countryside Code

### Be safe – plan ahead

Even when going out locally, it's best to get the latest information about where and when you can go; for example, your rights to go onto some areas of open land may be restricted while work is carried out, for safety reasons or during breeding and shooting seasons. Follow advice and local signs, and be prepared for the unexpected.

- Refer to up-to-date maps or guidebooks.
- You're responsible for your own safety and for others in your care, so be prepared for changes in weather and other events.
- There are many organisations offering specific advice on equipment and safety, or contact visitor information centres and libraries for a list of outdoor recreation groups.
- Check weather forecasts before you leave, and don't be afraid to turn back.
- Part of the appeal of the countryside is that you can get away from it all. You may not see anyone for hours and there are many places without clear mobile phone signals, so let someone else know where you're going and when you expect to return.

### Leave gates and property as you find them

Please respect the working life of the countryside, as our actions can affect people's livelihoods, our heritage, and the safety and welfare of animals and ourselves.

- A farmer will normally leave a gate closed to keep livestock in, but may sometimes leave it open so they can reach food and water. Leave gates as you find them or follow instructions on signs; if walking in a group, make sure the last person knows how to leave the gates.
- In fields where crops are growing, follow the paths wherever possible.
- Use gates and stiles wherever possible – climbing over walls, hedges and fences can damage them and increase the risk of farm animals escaping.
- Our heritage belongs to all of us – be careful not to disturb ruins and historic sites.
- Leave machinery and livestock alone – don't interfere with animals even if you think they're in distress. Try to alert the farmer instead.

### Protect plants and animals, and take your litter home

We have a responsibility to protect our countryside now and for future generations, so make sure you don't harm animals, birds, plants or trees.

- Litter and leftover food doesn't just spoil the beauty of the countryside, it can be dangerous to wildlife and farm animals and can spread disease – so take your litter home with you. Dropping litter and dumping rubbish are criminal offences.

- Discover the beauty of the natural environment and take special care not to damage, destroy or remove features such as rocks, plants and trees. They provide homes and food for wildlife, and add to everybody's enjoyment of the countryside.
- Wild animals and farm animals can behave unpredictably if you get too close, especially if they're with their young – so give them plenty of space.
- Fires can be as devastating to wildlife and habitats as they are to people and property – so be careful not to drop a match or smouldering cigarette at any time of the year. Sometimes, controlled fires are used to manage vegetation, particularly on heaths and moors between October and early April, so please check that a fire is not supervised before calling 999.

*Bee orchid*
*Photo: Kieron Huston*

**Keep dogs under close control**

The countryside is a great place to exercise dogs, but it is the owner's duty to make sure their dog is not a danger or nuisance to farm animals, wildlife or other people.

- By law, you must control your dog so that it does not disturb or scare farm animals or wildlife. You must keep your dog on a short lead on most areas of open country and common land between 1 March and 31 July, and at all times near farm animals.
- You do not have to put your dog on a lead on public paths as long as it is under close control. But as a general rule, keep your dog on a lead if you cannot rely on its obedience. By law, farmers are entitled to destroy a dog that injures or worries their animals.

- If a farm animal chases you and your dog, it is safer to let your dog off the lead – don't risk getting hurt by trying to protect it.
- Take particular care that your dog doesn't scare sheep and lambs or wander where it might disturb birds that nest on the ground and other wildlife – eggs and young will soon die without protection from their parents.
- Everyone knows how unpleasant dog mess is and it can cause infections – so always clean up after your dog and get rid of the mess responsibly. Also make sure your dog is wormed regularly.

**Consider other people**

Showing consideration and respect for other people makes the countryside a pleasant environment for everyone – at home, at work and at leisure.

- Busy traffic on small country roads can be unpleasant and dangerous to local people, visitors and wildlife – so slow down and, where possible, leave your vehicle at home, consider sharing lifts and use alternatives such as public transport or cycling. For public transport information, phone Traveline on 0871 200 2233.
- Respect the needs of local people – for example, don't block gateways, driveways or other entry points with your vehicle.
- By law, cyclists must give way to walkers and horse riders on bridleways.
- Keep out of the way when farm animals are being gathered or moved and follow directions from the farmer.
- Support the rural economy – for example, buy your supplies from local shops.

### Lyme Disease

An increasing problem, prevalent in the South East which can affect a small number of people very seriously. Any areas where deer or sheep have been grazing are particularly prone to this. Lyme disease is a bacterial infection that's spread to humans by infected ticks. Ticks are small, spider-shaped insects that feed on the blood of mammals, including humans. The most common symptom of Lyme disease is a red rash that looks similar to a bull's eye on a dart board. Left untreated, other symptoms can develop, including a high temperature (fever) – 38°C or higher, muscle pain, joint pain and swelling and neurological symptoms such as temporary paralysis of the facial muscles. A person with Lyme disease is not contagious because the infection can only be spread by the ticks. It's important to visit your doctor if you have been bitten by a tick, or if you have flu-like symptoms. Tell them that you suspect Lyme disease – it is easy to misdiagnose. Visit **www.nhs.uk** for more information.

## Maps, Descriptions, Distances

While every effort has been made to maintain accuracy within the maps and descriptions in this guide, we have had to process a vast amount of information and we are unable to guarantee that every single detail is correct.

Please exercise caution if a direction appears at odds with the route on the map. If in doubt, a comparison between the route, the description and a quick cross-reference with your map (along with a bit of common sense) should help ensure that you're on the right track. Note that distances have been measure on the map, and map distances rarely coincide 100 percent with distances on the ground. Please treat stated distances as a guideline only.

Ordnance Survey maps are the most commonly used, are easy to read and many people are happy using them – so they are what we have used here. If you're not familiar with OS maps and are unsure of what the symbols mean, you can download a free 1:25,000 map legend from **www.v-outdoor.co.uk**

See page xiii for a list of the OS maps covering the walks in this guide.

Here are a few of the symbols and abbreviations we use on the maps and in our directions:

 Refreshments     Start point

 Parking     Optional route

 Accessible by car     Direction of walk

 Accessible by bus     Accessible by train

## Km/mile conversion chart

### Metric to Imperial

| | | |
|---|---|---|
| 1 kilometre [km] | 1000 m | 0.6214 mile |
| 1 metre [m] | 100 cm | 1.0936 yd |

### Imperial to Metric

| | | |
|---|---|---|
| 1 mile | 1760 yd | 1.6093 km |
| 1 yard [yd] | 3 ft | 0.9144 m |
| 1 foot [ft] | 12 in | 0.3048 m |

*Bridleway marker on the Downs*

# Sussex Walks Area Map

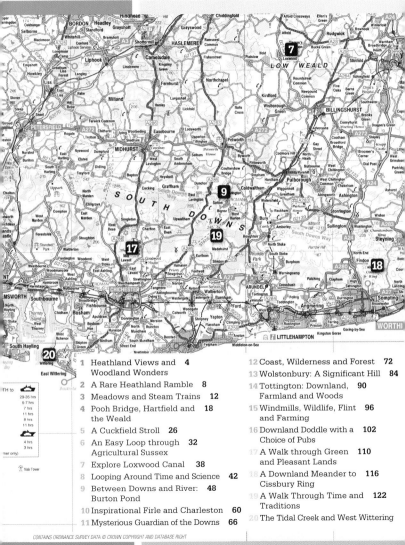

CONTAINS ORDNANCE SURVEY DATA © CROWN COPYRIGHT AND DATABASE RIGHT

# The Weald

The name 'Weald' has an old English ring to it. It means 'forest' or 'wood' but is nowadays used to refer to the tranche of land between the chalk escarpments of the North and South Downs. This land crosses several South Eastern counties, but we are interested in the Weald of Sussex. Once, this land would have been covered in extensive ancient forest, but changes in land use over time mean that you will now find a more diverse mix of geographical landscape. Despite this, the legacy of the ancient woodland is clear as Sussex remains one of the most 'wooded' counties in England.

The Weald is often divided into three main areas according to the soil type: the sandstone 'High Weald', the clay 'Low Weald' and the high points of the greensand ridge.

We classify our Wealden walks as either in the High Weald, (as defined by the Area of Outstanding Natural Beauty), or the Low Weald. The Cuckfield and Herstmonceux walks are both right on the border between the two.

*Burton Pond Reserve*

# High Weald and Ashdown Forest

The rolling hills, piecemeal fields and flower-rich grass land of the High Weald retain a mediaeval flavour. As you change direction to cross yet another small field, you are walking in the footsteps of early settlers who cleared fields of trees in an ad hoc fashion, contributing to its distinct character today. Look out for the 'shaws' (linear strips) or 'copses' which they left between fields, which today provide important wildlife corridors. Trees and woodland still cover about a third of the High Weald and over 70 percent of this is classed as ancient woodland because it's been in existence since 1600AD! This makes it an important home for those species who are slow to colonise new habitats, and also for archaeological features such as iron workings.

The Ashdown Forest is a particularly note-worthy area of the High Weald. This ancient area of tranquil and open heathland occupies an elevated position on the highest sandy ridge-top in the AONB. The expansive views still take me by surprise. You can stand on a ridge-top and gaze beyond open heath and over wealden woods towards the chalk escarpments of both the South and North Downs. The Forest is a former Royal Hunting Ground but has been used by commoners too, for activities such as grazing, iron working and fuel production for hearths and smelting. All these human endeavours left their mark on the Ashdown landscape, one way or another. Today, the Ashdown Forest is run by a Board of Conservators.

## Species of the Ashdown Forest

The unique heath and forest landscape of the Ashdown Forest make it a haven for a number of wildlife species. It is home to 34 butterfly species including the rare and elusive purple emperor and a number of moths such as common heath and the elephant hawk moth. Various small mammals reside here: common and pygmy shrew, the water shrew, the dormouse, the wood mouse and the yellow-necked mouse. Then there are all the usual suspects: foxes, rabbits, stoats, weasels, squirrels and badgers. Britain's only poisonous snake, the adder, can be found in the Ashdown Forest but unless you are very lucky(!), you are unlikely to see it sunning itself. This is of course another very good reason why dogs should be kept under close control! A large number of birds thrive in the area, either as permanent residents or as seasonal visitors, from the very large buzzard to the churring nightjar, drumming snipe or perhaps a brambling perched on the edge of Five Hundred Acre Wood.

*Adder*

# 1 Heathland Views and Woodland Wonders

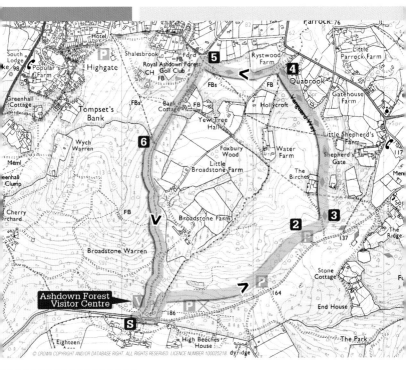

Enjoy far-reaching ridge-top views as you traverse fabulous Ashdown Forest heathland, then follow the Vanguard Way down through woods before wandering back through wonderful Broadstone Warren woodland.

**CREATIVE
STARTING POINTS**

- Colour and detail
- Texture and shape
- Far and near
- Strength, action
  and fragility

*Broadstone Warren, Ashdown Forest*

**START** Ashdown Forest Visitor Centre entrance/noticeboard/assembly point.

**GRID REF** TQ 432 323

**TOTAL ASCENT** 471 ft/143 m

**PARKING** Visitor Centre car park (signed from crossroads at Wych Cross by the garden centre).

**PUBLIC TRANSPORT**
*Metrobus service* 291 from East Grinstead to Tunbridge Wells and 270 from East Grinstead to Haywards Heath. *Stagecoach service* 54 runs from Eastbourne to East Grinstead.
*www.metrobus.co.uk*
*www.stagecoachbus.com*

**TERRAIN** Mainly mud paths through heath and woodland with moderate gradients. Dogs under control in Ashdown Forest.

**REFRESHMENTS** Ashdown Park Hotel opposite start. Treat yourself to a posh lunch – change of muddy gear recommended. Pre-booking advised, *T* 01342 824988.
*www.ashdownpark.com*

**OS MAP** Explorer 135: Ashdown Forest

In summer, Broadstone Heath welcomes breeding birds such as the dartford warbler, nightjar, stonechat and tree pipit. The heath is also home to reptiles such as the common lizard, slow worm, grass snake and adder. The lizards form the main prey of the adders as few small mammals live on the heath. In wetter areas, look out for heathland plants such as round-leaved sundew, bog asphodel and bog cotton.

**S** TQ 432 323 The visitor centre has toilets and offers interesting displays and information about the Ashdown Forest.

Follow the footpath away from the road (north) into the trees in the direction of the Ashdown Forest marker post. The woodland path follows the line of a wire fence. At the second Ashdown Forest marker post, walk **right** and enjoy breath-taking views to the left, over Broadstone Heath to the North Downs.

Stay on this wide ride, the 'Ridge Road'. **Ignore** the left fork shortly before the Millennium Clump of Scots pines, planted in 2000. Glimpse a car park towards the road. Keep on the wide ride. Pass a second car park. The path leads you into woods. See Townsends car park on your right. At the fork, **walk left** towards open heath.

**2** TQ 443 329 At the bench, turn **right**. Your path runs through trees. Cross the red brick and gravel driveway to **continue walking straight ahead**. Stay on this track until you reach Vanguard Way.

Broadstone Heath

**5.6 km / 3.5 miles**

**3** TQ 445 330 Turn **left** along Vanguard Way/the horse route (there's a small VW sign on the marker post in the far right corner). Walk down the slope. Vanguard Way is joined by a gravelly track. Keep walking **straight ahead**. The path continues downward. See a large house over to the left. At the T-junction, turn **left**. Walk past a rough wooden fence. See the same house over to your left. Walk **straight across** the brick and gravel crossroads and up the grassy ride opposite. Soon reach a grassy cross-roads. Turn **right** and follow the path which runs roughly parallel to golfing greens.

**4** TQ 441 341 Emerge onto the Royal Ashdown Forest Golf Course. Follow the Vanguard Way **straight ahead**. Go over the footbridge. Pass the VW marker post before the driveway. Keep walking **straight ahead**. Cross the next fairway. Keep walking. Cross the gravel path at the pond and walk **straight on** along the line of the trees.

**5** TQ 436 342 At the tarmac track, turn **left** along the (here unsigned) public footpath. Walk past the houses and Bank Cottage Farm, heading south-west. Follow the grassy track **straight ahead** along the edge of the trees.

**6** TQ 432 337 The footpath leads you away from the golf course through Broadstone Warren Woods, heading **south** back to the visitor centre. The track splits. Take the **left** fork, heading south-east. Bear **left** at the yellow arrow. Turn **right** along the tarmac track. You'll be glad of the hard-surface as the track climbs steadily. Pass the ranger buildings. At the road, turn **left** and walk 50m along to the visitor centre car park and entrance.

*This is a public footpath through private woodland owned by the Scout Association. There are some simply beautiful trees here: ancient oaks, huge old beech trees, scots pine … Fallen branches and trees are a part of the woodland floor. They're not forgotten but providing sustenance to woodland invertebrates. The sun leaps through gaps in the canopy as your path wends its way onwards, climbing gradually.*

## 2 A Rare Heathland Ramble

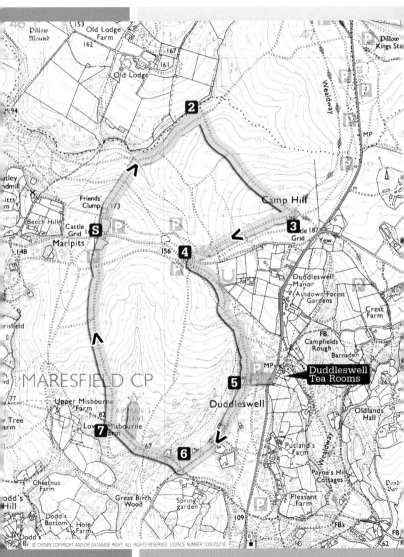

© CROWN COPYRIGHT AND/OR DATABASE RIGHT. ALL RIGHTS RESERVED. LICENCE NUMBER 100025218.

*Heathland*

An exhilarating walk around ancient and rugged heathland, stopping at a charming tea shop for refreshments and offering a wonderful feeling of space and far-reaching views from the sandy ridge-top of the High Weald Area of Outstanding Natural Beauty.

### CREATIVE STARTING POINTS

- Reflections and distortions
- Common, communal and solitary
- Horizon and focal points
- Jagged or smooth

**START** at *The Great Wall of Ashdown* noticeboard by the 'Friends' clump of trees.
**GRID REF** TQ 456 288
**TOTAL ASCENT** 612 ft/187 m
**PARKING** Friends car park, Crowborough Road, off the A22 just North of Nutle.

**TERRAIN** A lack of marked tracks can make this area tricky to navigate. Rugged ground with some slopes. Many grazing animals – dogs on leads/under close control.
**REFRESHMENTS** Duddleswell Tea Rooms. Closed winter/Tues/Weds, *T* 01825 712126.
**OS MAP** Explorer 135: Ashdown Forest

# 2 A Rare Heathland Ramble

*Tree Clumps are a feature of the Ashdown Forest. The 'Friends' clump here was planted by The Friends of Ashdown Forest in 1973, to commemorate 'The Year of the Tree.' Clumps of Scots pines were first ordered to be planted by Elizabeth, Countess de la Warr back in 1825. The clumps are certainly handy for navigation.*

*This area has been used as a military training ground in WW1 (for practice trenches) and WW2 (for tanks). More information on the military history is available at the Ashdown Forest Centre.*

*At Camp Hill Clump there are benches, viewpoints and a trig point. This clump was first planted in 1825 and it's thought that the name derives from a military camp hereabouts back in July 1793. There are signs of old 'field kitchens' in the vicinity.*

*On a good day, you can see the distant South Downs around Firle Beacon about 16 miles to the south.*

**S** TQ 456 288 Walk **straight ahead** beyond the clump, the bench and down the long slope on the wide path. Walk on through the copse at the bottom of the dip and continue **straight ahead** on the other side. The path is unmarked and consists of several narrow tracks running parallel to the trees. The path rises.

**2** TQ 462 296 **Easy-to-miss:** As the path starts to slope downwards, look for a small lone evergreen tree and turn **right** along the unsigned wide grassy path opposite two similar trees (if you reach the footbridge across the brook you've gone too far). Walk up the short steep slope and **straight ahead** to the top of the hill. Note various clumps of trees on your left and Camp Hill Clump on the horizon ahead.

**3** TQ 469 289 Reach Camp Hill Clump. Turn **right** along the first turning with the small rickety WW post. Walk on for some way. Pass Ellison's Pond and go through the car park.

**4** TQ 461 286 Cross the road to Hollies car park. At the wooden way-mark signpost, go **left** following the wide grassy footpath. It curves round towards a ridge with far-reaching views.

Continue down a slope. Walk through a small clump of trees and continue **straight on**. At the unsigned fork, keep to the **right-hand side**, walking **straight ahead**. The path leads you through a small wood. Continue on until you reach a broken, tarmac path.

**5** TQ 465 278
**OPTIONAL ROUTE** To divert 200m to Duddleswell cafe, turn **left** to walk to the road. Go through the gate.

Turn **left** along the road, passing Duddleswell car park and cross the road to Duddleswell Tea Rooms. Return to the gate but instead of going back through it, walk diagonally **left** following the signed footpath along the long grassy path through the hinged gate, almost doubling-back on yourself.

**MAIN ROUTE**  To continue on our main route, go **straight across** the broken tarmac path and walk **straight ahead** with the trees on your right. Soon there are trees on both sides. Stay on this wide path. Cross a tarmac driveway and walk **straight on**. The track becomes rougher and slopes downwards.

**6**  TQ 461 272 At the crossroads by the oak tree, turn **right** along the footpath. The path slopes upwards and opens out. See the white house on your distant right. **Keep going.** Walk past the farm. Take the **left fork** and go down the slope. Keep following the mud track. It runs through heath and woods. Look out for the wooden footbridges in the hollow of the copse.

**OPTIONAL ROUTE**  Turn **right** here to divert to the Airman's Grave. **Return** to previous path.

**MAIN ROUTE**  Walk **straight on**, heading west.

**7**  TQ 456 275 Easy-to-miss: at the brow of the hill where the trees are, **follow the path round to the right** heading north. It's an uphill stretch but there are magnificent views across the heathland. At the top as you approach the road, head for the bench. See your car park and the Friends clump of trees ahead. Cross the road back to your car.

*Heathland is one of our rarest and most threatened habitats. Only about 15 percent of the heathland that existed in 1815 now remains and the Ashdown Forest contains a staggering three percent of the remaining heathland in Britain! It is the largest area of lowland heath in the South East, a habitat characterised by land at altitudes below 300 metres where plants from the ericaceae family, such as heathers and dwarf shrubs dominate. There tend to be few trees. Significantly, heathland is a 'plagioclimax' vegetation type. This means that it evolves through human activity and it generally needs human activity to maintain it, for example, through livestock grazing.*

*This is a memorial to the young crew of a Wellington bomber which crashed here when forced to turn back in stormy weather on a bombing trip to Cologne.*

# 3 Meadows and Steam Trains

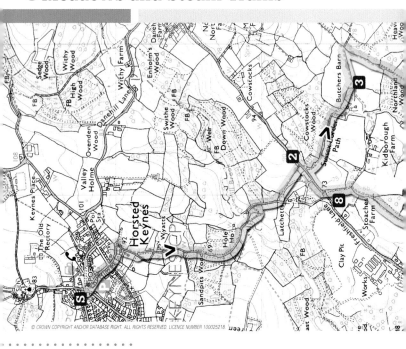

A wonderful walk which starts with the easy-walking Sussex Border Path and goes on to explore woodland and summer meadows peppered with orchids. The route passes within waving distance of steam trains (when running) and there's a lovely pub at the half-way point.

## 10.4 km / 6.4 miles

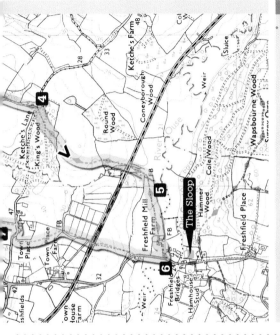

**CREATIVE STARTING POINTS**

- Fast or slow
- Direction versus random movement
- Diverging or converging lines
- One or many

**START** Horsted Keynes Rural Car Park.
**GRID REF** TQ 383 281
**TOTAL ASCENT** 598 ft/182 m
**PARKING** Horsted Keynes Rural Car Park beside Horsted Club and post office.
**PUBLIC TRANSPORT** Not easy
**TERRAIN** Long stretches of hard-surfaced border path plus grassy paths. Some grassy paths between **points 4**

and **6** are unclear, but the detailed directions should help.

**REFRESHMENTS** The Sloop Inn in Freshfield, *T* 01444 831219, or a picnic whilst watching the trains. The Green Man in Horsted Keynes, *T* 01825 790656.

**OS MAP** Explorer 135: Ashdown Forest

# 3 Meadows and Steam Trains

*The Bluebell Railway, a standard gauge passenger line, has survived a some-what chequered battle for preservation. Back in 1882, the original Lewes and East Grinstead Railway Line was opened to much celebration, aiming to provide 'four passenger trains each way daily … with through connections at East Grinstead to London, and stop at Sheffield Bridges, Newick and West Hoathly' (according to the Schedule of the 1877 and 1878 Act). Why were such rural spots chosen for stations by this private company? Perhaps because the promoters included not only the Earl of Sheffield of Sheffield Park but also the well-heeled residents of Newick Park and Reeden. A line extension to East Grinstead is to open in 2013.*

*It's always a pleasure to come across a wildflower meadow when you're out walking. Once, such meadows were associated with clearings in woods but, as humans began to clear land for farming, these grasslands became more widespread and were commonly used for grazing and harvesting hay. In recent years, traditional hay meadows and pastures have suffered from extremes: either being 'left-alone' or intensively managed with many grasslands having been treated and re-sown.*

**S** **TQ 383 282** Exit the car park past Horsted Club. Turn **right** along the signed West Sussex Border Path. Walk **straight ahead** along Wyatts Lane, following the West Sussex Border Path. Pass a selection of large houses and stay on the signed West Sussex Border Path, **ignoring** a couple of footpaths which join it. Walk **straight ahead** through Sandpits Wood. (**Ignore** the footpath leading right.) The path emerges from woods to run beside a field. Follow the signed Border Path **left** and go **right** at the tarmac driveway, still following the Border Path. Walk up a short, sharp slope. Veer **left** on the signed grassy bridleway, leaving the Tarmac lane.

**2** **TQ 392 267** At the road, turn **right** to walk along the grass verge. Almost immediately, turn **left** along the public footpath towards Butchers Barn. This tarmac path continues for some time. Pass Keepers Cottage and soon head **left** to leave the tarmac path, cross the stile marked by a yellow arrow and to follow the footpath through the meadow.

**3** **TQ 397 263** At the signpost, walk **left**. In the top (east) corner of the field, there's an unsigned gap in the hedge. Go **right**, through this gap, cutting through to the footpath. Walk away from the stile, (**without** crossing it), following the Border Path along the fence. At the corner of the field, cross the stile and follow the yellow arrow **right**.

Follow the path through the coppiced woods and then along the fence. *Look out for some wonderful fox-glove displays.* Follow the signed footpath ahead. *You may hear the odd toot!* Pass a house and again, at the signpost, walk **straight ahead** along the path. Pass Kingswood Cottage.

**4**  TQ 395 253 Cross Ketche's Lane and follow the footpath opposite. There's a broken sign here and a rough fork, but the path you want immediately curves to the **right** and wends its way through the woods. Emerge into an open field. Walk **straight ahead** as signed by the arrow. The path is unclear. Head for the right side of the circular thicket where you may spot a hide, pond and, most importantly, a signpost sticking up out of the ferns. Keep walking **diagonally right** through the long grass. Reach a post in the hedge and see the Bluebell Railway signal post in the distance. There's a copse on your right hiding another wooden waymarker. Walk **ahead** along the track between field and copse. As you approach the track, veer **right** along the path to pass through a tunnel beneath the railway.

*There are several types of grassland, each characterised by its soil type: neutral, acidic or chalk. This soil type affects which plants will grow, which in turn affects the wildlife the land supports, such as butterflies. This particular meadow is a 'neutral grassland' associated with clay and silty soils. Look out for the common spotted orchid, abundant here in summer months. Neutral grassland tends to attract butterflies such as common blue and meadow brown. (The following walks all pass through chalk grassland: A Downland Meander to Cissbury Ring; Coast, Wilderness and Forest; Wolstonbury: A Significant Hill; Ditchling Beacon in both Downland Doddle and Windmills, Wildlife, Flint and Farming).*

*Bluebell Railway*

## 3 Meadows and Steam Trains

This is a good vantage point
for the Bluebell Railway.
There are hammer ponds
and forge sites near the
Bluebell. Iron was made in
the Weald from pre-Roman
times until the beginning
of the 19th century.

**5** **TQ 391 247** Go through a gate and walk **straight ahead** along an unclear grassy path. Head **right** across a stream and through a gate. Follow the Sussex Border Path **straight ahead**. Cross the footbridge. Head for the farm buildings. Go across the gated footbridge and walk **straight ahead** to cross the stile. Head **diagonally left** across one last field.

**6** **TQ 385 244** Walk **left** to visit The Sloop pub.

To continue on, walk **right** along the road. Look for the stile beside the metal gate. Cross this and climb across a second and a third stile on your left. Keep walking **left** to go **straight up** the field to the railway bridge.

Cross the bridge, following the signed footpath **straight ahead** between two fences. At the next sign, walk **left** across the footbridge. Head up **diagonally left** across the field following the signpost. Pass another signpost at the corner of the hedged property. Keep following the signed footpath until you reach the road.

**7** **TQ 386 255** Head **right** very briefly along the road. After Town Place, walk **left** through the kissing gate and follow the footpath. At the end of the field, go through another couple of kissing gates, passing Bluebell Vineyard Estates on your right. Walk on through the woods, along the side of a meadow. Enter some more woods. Turn **left** when you hit the footpath at the signpost.

**8** **TQ 390 265** Reach Freshfield Lane, opposite Latchetts. Walk **right**. Look for the Sussex Border Path leading **left** to retrace your earlier footsteps back to Horsted Keynes.

*Common spotted orchid in neutral grassland*

# 4 Pooh Bridge, Hartfield and the Weald

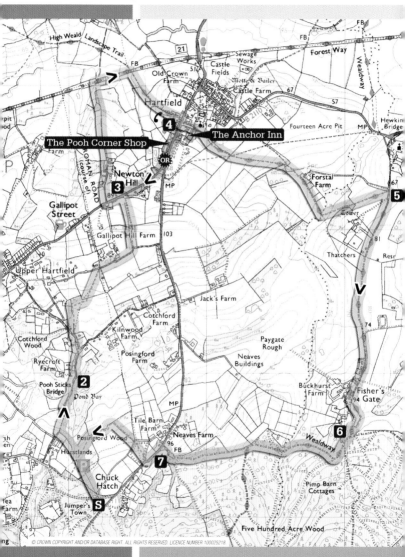

High Weald Landscape Trail

21

FB

FB

Forest Way

Wealdway

Sewage Works

Old Crown Farm

Castle Fields

Motte & Bailey Castle Farm

67

57

Hewkin Bridge

Hartfield

School

Fourteen Acre Pit

MP

4

The Anchor Inn

The Pooh Corner Shop

ROMAN ROAD (course of)

OR

Forstal Farm

5

Newton Hill

3

MP

Gallipot Street

Lower

Thatchers

81

Resr

Gallipot Hill Farm

103

Upper Hartfield

Jack's Farm

74

Cotchford Farm

Kilnwood Farm

Paygate Rough

Cotchford Wood

Posingford Farm

Neaves Buildings

Ryecroft Farm

Buckhurst Farm

Fisher's Gate

94

Pooh Sticks Bridge

2

Pond Bay

MP

Tile Barn Farm

96 FB

Neaves Farm

6

Posingford Wood

Hurstlands

7

Wealdway

Chuck Hatch

Pimp Barn Cottages

Jumper's Town

S

Five Hundred Acre Wood

A pleasant walk which begins near Pooh Sticks Bridge and passes through Hartfield, with its pubs and Pooh Corner shop/cafe. From Hartfield, you may either return to the bridge or continue past the church and through the wild and peaceful Buckhurst Estate to join the Wealdway along the edge of the Hundred Acre Woods. Very young families may just want to visit the bridge!

**CREATIVE STARTING POINTS**

- Competition versus cooperation
- Barriers, break, bridge
- Shape and motion
- Signs and illustration

**START** Pooh car park.
**GRID REF** TQ 472 332
**TOTAL ASCENT** 691 ft/211 m
**PARKING** Pooh car park, Chuck Hatch Lane off Cotchford Hill, B2026.
**PUBLIC TRANSPORT**
*Bus Metrobus* 291 from East Grinstead to Tunbridge Wells stops in Hartfield.

**TERRAIN** Some hard-surfaced bridleways and some grassy, meadow and mud tracks which may be boggy when wet. Dogs on lead through Buckhurst Estate.
**REFRESHMENTS** The Hay Waggon, *T* 01892 770 252, the Anchor Inn, *T* 01892 770 424, and Pooh Corner shop and cafe (with WC), *T* 01892 770 456, are all in Hartfield. Or a picnic in the churchyard?
**OS MAP** Explorer 135: Ashdown Forest

# 4 Pooh Bridge, Hartfield and the Weald

**S** TQ 472 332 At the far end of the car park, go through the gates and immediately see a marker post labelled Bridge. Follow the sign, walking **straight ahead** on the bridleway. Pass some benches.

At the next two wooden waymarker signposts, continue **straight ahead** on the bridleway. Cross a footbridge (not Pooh Bridge!) and walk on as signed. Turn **right** at the next signed post. Stay on this track and you will soon reach Pooh Bridge.

**2** TQ 470 338 Walk **straight ahead**. At the tarmac path, walk **right**. Almost immediately, go **left** where the signed bridleway forks. Look for the stile just beyond the walled house. Go **right** along the footpath to Hartfield. Walk up the field and cross another stile. Head onwards and upwards, being sure to pause and look back at the beautiful vista. Cross over the stile and go through the kissing gate opposite to follow the narrow footpath ahead. **Easy to miss:** Leave this track to walk **left** along the footpath at the post/yellow arrow. Reach the B2110 road.

**3** TQ 473 352 Turn **left** and walk along the pavement for a short distance. At Landhurst Gate Lodge, cross the road to turn **right** along the bridleway. Walk past the house and on through the farm buildings. The track now runs between a hedge and a field. See Hartfield church spire to your right. Keep walking. Go through the metal gate and into the woods (this section of path can be muddy if wet). Go through the metal gate and walk across the beautiful grassland glade to the next metal gate. Walk up the steps of the old embankment to turn **right** along railway trail, Forest Way, for a short way.

Just after a picnic bench, turn **right** to cross a stile and join the (here unmarked) High Weald Landscape Trail. Walk **straight ahead**, eventually crossing a stile into Hartfield Recreation ground. Walk past the tennis courts.

**4** **TQ 478 357** At the road, turn right for shop, Pooh Corner and choice of two pubs.

**OPTIONAL ROUTE** For a short cut back to the car park, continue **straight** past Pooh Corner shop. When the road forks, keep **right**. Look out for the earlier footpath leading **left** back to Pooh Bridge.

**MAIN ROUTE** To follow our main route, walk **right**, passing the Anchor Inn to turn **left** up Church Street. The road soon turns into a footpath which leads you past the rather stunning church of St Mary *(a few handy benches make the churchyard a popular picnic/rest spot with walkers)*. Beside the church, go **right** up the steps and across the stile to continue in the same direction, following the High Weald Landscape Trail towards Withyam. Cross another couple of stiles and keep walking. You are entering Buckhurst Estate *(dogs on leads!)*.

Follow the long-grass path. At the signpost, go diagonally **right** to keep walking in roughly the same direction. Go through the gateposts and take the **left** grassy fork along the hedge then fence.

Cross the bridge and turn **left**, leaving the track to follow the public footpath along the stream and up through the woods. Pass a stile and keep walking **straight ahead** through another grassland meadow. Head up towards the far corner (to the left of the fenced utilities) where there's a stile to cross.

*Pooh Bridge was made famous by A.A.Milne's famous Winnie-the-Pooh books and people come from all over the world to see it – and to play 'Pooh Sticks.'*

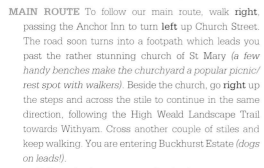

*This is an area rich in wildlife. A hare crossed my path, pausing to sunbathe – keep your eyes peeled!*

# 4 Pooh Bridge, Hartfield and the Weald

*You may choose to divert at the top of the hill through Hundred Acre Woods, rejoining us where we leave the Wealdway. Despite its name, less than 40 percent of the Ashdown Forest is woodland, now carefully managed by the Ashdown Forest Conservators. Look out for the beautiful beech pollards in this wood. Pollarding is a form of coppicing where the cutting occurs above the height of grazing animals. These trees haven't been pollarded for over 100 years and would probably not survive being cut now.*

**5** TQ 493 352 Turn **right** onto the Wealdway. Follow this private road for a mile (1.5 km) until you have passed through cottages and reach Fisher's Gate house itself. By the white gate, go **left** over the stile and along the footpath. Follow the fence round and soon cross a stile. Continue on a narrow path then driveway.

**6** TQ 490 335 Walk **straight ahead** across the driveway to the house at the crossroads. Keep **right** staying on the Wealdway and ignoring several offshoots. The track turns into a mud path. Keep walking **straight ahead** along the fence, leaving the Wealdway as it veers left just before you go downhill, where you keep **right**.

Stay on this track through the edge of the Hundred Acre Wood. Cross a footbridge then veer **right** and upwards away from the stream, following the track between banks.

**7** TQ 476 335 At the road, walk **left** along the verge for a short distance. Just before you reach Forest Ridge House, cross to go **right**. Follow the signed footpath across the stile. Follow the public footpath through or around the sand school as per signs. Cross the stile and follow the footpath **right**. At the signpost go **left** along the grassy footpath. Cross another stile and follow path into woods. Head **left** back to your car as you join the bridleway between the car park and Pooh Bridge.

Hartfield track

# The Low Weald

As the name suggests, the Low Weald tends to be low-lying! In general, this ancient area was cleared and settled before the High Weald, vanquishing much of the Low Wealden forest and leaving wide clay vales or valleys. These are still dotted with small woodlands and fields, but the Low Weald has an open feel to it.

Clay is a dominant feature of the gently undulating landscape – as perhaps, are boggy fields: surface-water is very much in evidence! Ponds, meandering streams and marshy carr are all features of our Low Weald walks. Sussex residents have capitalized on these wetland features for industry (the Iron Age hammer pond at Burton) and even made their own waterways (Loxwood Canal). Walk the towpath and see how Sussex wildlife benefits from this watery habitat today. The streams you hear babbling or see puddling over your path help drain the Weald, eventually leading to rivers such as the Mole, Rother and Ouse. Look out for the flood plains – areas of low-lying ground adjacent to rivers that provide a vital function by giving excess flood water somewhere to flow.

Sussex is a highly agricultural county and, by walking through the countryside, we can connect with where our food comes from. Agriculture occupies about two-thirds of the county's land and so the majority of its wildlife lives on farms. Farming methods have changed rapidly in the last half-century and there has been a growing awareness of the impact of agricultural land-use on wildlife and the enviroment.

*Agricultural wealden land*

# 5 A Cuckfield Stroll

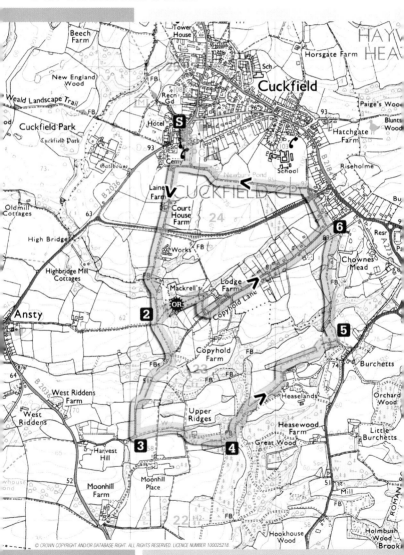

The 'field' in the name 'Cuckfield' is a Saxon ending, meaning 'a clearing where forest trees were felled'. Perched on the edge of the High Weald AONB, this historic village has houses dating back to the 14th century and the surrounding landscape has a true 'wealden' feel to it. This leisurely walk leads you through woodland, alongside streams which were once the site of Iron-Age workings and past tucked away houses in the heart of rural Sussex.
(An easy short cut is available).

### CREATIVE STARTING POINTS

- Pathways and signposts
- Lost, found, waiting
- Sunbursts and puddles
- Rhythm and shape

**START** Entrance to Church Street, Cuckfield.
**GRID REF** TQ 303 245 (parking at TQ 304 246)
**TOTAL ASCENT** 414 ft/126 m
**PARKING** Broad Street car park (use a Mid Sussex parking disc, available from various high street establishments). Turn left out of the car park and left along the high street at the mini-roundabout.

**PUBLIC TRANSPORT**
*Bus* A bus timetable is available through Cuckfield parish Council.
*www.cuckfield.gov.uk*
*Train* The nearest station is Haywards Heath.
**TERRAIN** Easy. A mix of mainly level soft and hard surfaces. Puddle at stream ford.
**REFRESHMENTS** There's a good choice of cafés and pubs in Cuckfield.
**OS MAP** Explorer 135: Ashdown Forest

## 5 A Cuckfield Stroll

*The current building of the Church of Holy Trinity dates from the 13th century, but the earliest recorded mention of the church was in 1092 when a Norman building would have existed. It's a very tranquil spot to stop and pause for thought.*

*In the mid-16th century, iron production became Cuckfield's most profitable industry. This area was perfect for development as an iron-workings and a dam was built to power a water-wheel and there were a number of hammer ponds along this stream. The furnace and forge in this area were owned by Sir Walter Covert, one of Cuckfield's most prominent families. Find out more at Cuckfield Museum www.cuckfield.org*

**S** TQ 303 245 Turn **left** along Church Street. Walk **straight ahead** through the lychgate and along the tarmac path through Holy Trinity Church graveyard.

Go through the iron kissing gate and turn **right** along the track. At the wooden way marker, follow the footpath left along the unmade road. Walk **straight on** through Court House Farm (there's a kiosk selling eggs). Continue **straight ahead**, passing the waymarker post. Cross the stile.

Cross the busy(!) road. Follow the signed public footpath through two metal kissing gates and **straight ahead** across the field. Go through the kissing gate into the next field and walk down the gentle slope, passing the footpath sign.

Pass beside or cross the stile and walk down into the copse, following the mud track. Cross the footbridge and follow the track as it curves left and then wends its way up through the trees. Pass a footpath sign and emerge at Mackrell's, a timber-framed house.

Follow the grassy track **right**. Walk across the wooden-planked 'bridge' over the stream to continue along the drive. There's a tree plantation to your left.

**2** TQ 301 233 Reach a waymarker sign shortly before the track bends.

**SHORT CUT** For a short cut via Copyhold Lane, follow the track **left** through the trees, doubling back on yourself. Reach a waymarker and continue on down the steep wood-edged steps. Cross the footbridge over the stream and follow the path up the slope and to the waymarker sign and five-bar gate. Go **straight ahead** through the gate. At the pond and signpost, turn **right**. Cross the stile and walk up the slope, following the signpost along

*Look out for glimpses of the South Downs across the Low Weald.*

the fenced path. Emerge onto a hard-surfaced path. Turn **left** along Copyhold Lane. Where the footpath crosses the road at the stile and two sign posts, rejoin our route at **point 6**, turning **left** off Copyhold Lane along the narrow signed footpath

**MAIN ROUTE** To continue on our main walk, follow the direction of the waymarker pointing **straight ahead**, leaving the drive-way to reach a nearby second signpost. Cross the stile to walk **left** between the field and the trees. At the next wooden waymarker, **veer left** into the copse. *There's a wild feel to this copse which has a stream tumbling through its centre.* Cross the footbridge and walk on a small distance. At the bridleway, turn **right**. Pass Old Furnace Cottage and **ignore** the footpath on your left, following the bridleway **straight ahead** between the fences. This muddy bridleway leads up past a big oak tree and along traditional hedgerow, passing another waymarker sign to reach the metal gate. Follow the signed bridleway **straight ahead**.

3 **TQ 300 225** At the next wooden waymarker sign, follow the mud footpath **left** along the edge of the field. At the next sign, continue **straight ahead**, following the footpath through the next field. Reach a T-junction with a track and a three-way sign. Turn **right** to walk up a short slope. Pass the house 'Upper Ridges'. Follow the signed but not obvious footpath which leads **left** across the field, initially diagonally. Walk with the front of Upper Ridges some way to your left as you follow the (invisible) footpath across the field. Head for the wooden waymarker sign beside the lone tree in the middle of the field. Walk across the field towards the far stile, avoiding the low electric fence as necessary.

# 5 A Cuckfield Stroll

**4** TQ 306 225 Cross the stile and walk **straight ahead** following the signed public footpath. Cross the bridge over the stream and at the sign, walk **left** up the slope. Head past the next wooden sign to follow the footpath up through the trees.

Walk through the gate into the field (dogs on leads please). Follow the footpath **straight ahead**. Go through the wooden gate and on through a small grazing area. **Veer left**, following the old wooden sign which points left, to the metal kissing gate. Go through and **continue diagonally** across the next field to the wooden way-marker post. Turn **right** to walk along the field boundary. Go through the next metal kissing gate and walk along the fence, then follow the signed footpath across the field. Walk through the open gateposts.

**5** TQ 314 231 At the three-way wooden waymarker, turn **left**, following the footpath. Cross the stile and head into the woods. At the top of a short hill, go over

the stile and follow the footpath sign **straight ahead**. Pass mid-field scrub and continue past two large oaks towards the stile beside the metal gate. Climb over and walk on. At the signpost, cross the next stile and follow the footpath **diagonally right**. Cross yet another stile and a tarmac driveway to follow a grassy footpath straight ahead for a very short distance. Cross another stile and Copyhold Lane.

**THE SHORT CUT REJOINS HERE**

6    **TQ 313 239** Follow the narrow signed footpath. Walk the short distance along the fence to cross the stile and busy(!) road, then walk along the signed footpath opposite. At the wooden waymarker, turn **left** to follow the footpath beside the school fields. Pass a waymarker sign, cross the stile and walk **straight ahead** along the edge of the field. Cross the next stile to follow the footpath onwards past Newbury Pond. Turn **right** back into the churchyard and the start.

*On your left, see distant South Downs beyond the High Weald.*

*Cuckfield stroll*

# 6 An Easy Loop through Agricultural Sussex

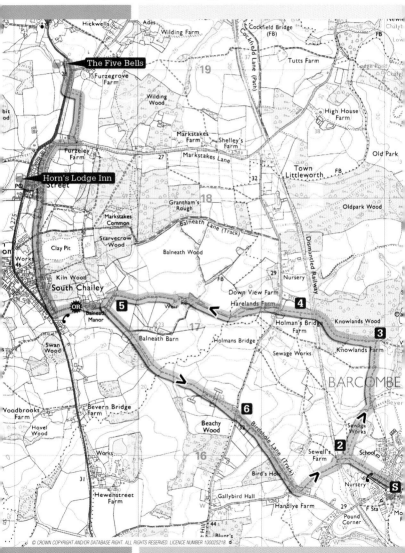

### 6.9 km / 4.25 miles or 12.2 km / 7.5 miles

*Bluebells in wood*

This flat walk links two Sussex villages via an organic farm (with shop), a beautiful woodland and varied agricultural paths, with an optional extension to two welcoming pubs.

**CREATIVE STARTING POINTS**
- Sharp, soft
- Across, over or under
- Nurture, protect, nourish
- Stone, wood or earth

**START** Barcombe Post Office.
**GRID REF** TQ 420 157
**TOTAL ASCENT** 305 ft/92 m
**PARKING** Barcombe car park (free), next to Barcombe Stores and Post Office.
**PUBLIC TRANSPORT** No buses currently run to Barcombe.

**TERRAIN** Flat with a mix of hard-surfaced, grass and mud tracks.
**REFRESHMENTS** Buy a picnic at the Farm Shop or from Barcombe Post Office. There's also plenty on offer in the pubs in Chailey.
**OS MAP** Explorer 122: Brighton and Hove

# 6 An Easy Loop through Agricultural Sussex

*Walking and chatting*

### 6.9 km / 4.25 miles or 12.2 km / 7.5 miles

**S** **TQ 420 157** Cross the road and walk **left**. Immediately look **right** for a small track, Grange Road and turn up this. Walk past the five bar gate and continue **straight ahead** through Barcombe Recreation Ground. Pass the gate to Pump House Field, a community green space. Continue between the tennis courts and tennis club summerhouse. Go on past the bike jumps. Walk down the wood-edged steps and cross the footbridge.

**2** **TQ 417 159** Walk **right**, along the stream following the footpath across the field. Cross the stile with metal bars and walk **straight on**. Head for the gate, unfastening the chain. Walk on and turn **left**. Go through two yellow arrow-marked gates on both sides of the bridge across Bevern stream. Continue **straight ahead** to the metal gate. Cross the stile and walk **straight on**. When you reach the footbridge/stile and sign, cross and continue **straight ahead**. Go through the stile-gate. See the red-tiled/timber-framed buildings on your right.

**3** **TQ 419 168** Turn **left** through the gate along the mud track. You are walking through the private nature reserve, Knowlands Wood.

Keep walking **straight ahead** on the track following the public footpath signs. Go through the old railway tunnel and across the stile. Walk on and immediately see a stile on your left. Go **left**, crossing the stile. Walk **straight on** along the hedge. Cross the stile and walk **right** on the concrete footpath. Pass Holmansbridge Farm Shop, the Smokehouse Lewes and Beal's Charcuterie – or stop for ice-cream, or to buy local bread and smoked fish or charcuterie to make a picnic.
*www.holmansbridgefarm.com*

*Knowlands Wood is a beautiful tranquil woodland. This is a privately-owned nature reserve, so please treat it with due respect. Keep all dogs strictly on leads.*

# 6 An Easy Loop through Agricultural Sussex

4   TQ 411 171 Cross the road and then the stile. Walk
    **straight ahead** across the field. Go through the gate
    and walk along beside the hedge. *See distant Lewes
    down on your left.* Enter the wood and go **right** at the
    fork, taking the unsigned footpath. See the yellow arrow
    on the gatepost before the field? Go **left** along the narrow
    mud track through a pleasant copse. Cross the foot
    bridges over the streams. Follow the mud track as it runs
    for some time along the fenced grazing fields. You will
    need to cross a couple of stiles.

5   TQ 397 171
OPTIONAL ROUTE For an add-on to a choice of nice
    pubs, walk **straight ahead**. Go almost as far as the
    road but not quite. Go **right** along an unsigned stony
    public byway. Cross the road which leads into small
    housing estate. Walk alongside the fence. Keep going
    **straight ahead**. Walk across the bridge over the quarry.
    Pass a waymarker sign and walk **straight ahead**
    through the concrete bollards and onwards. Pass the
    gated entrance to Caveridge Farmhouse.

    For **Horn's Lodge Inn** (CAMRA pub of the year,
    10.2 km total walk), **walk left** at Setfords Field road.
    Pass the small block of flats and turn **left** down narrow
    unsigned tarmac path between block of flats and
    fence. Follow zigzagging path right and left and then
    at the main road, turn right to Horns Lodge Inn and the
    village shop.

    For the **Five Bells** (12.2 km total walk), keep **straight
    ahead**, passing Setfords Field road and walk on to the
    end of Green Lane. Turn **right** along Markstakes Lane
    for roughly 50 metres. At the wooden sign, turn **left**
    along the footpath. There's an unusual gated stile which
    you must either climb or squeeze past if you're thin

**6.9 km / 4.25 miles or 12.2 km / 7.5 miles**

At the tall footpath sign, walk **straight ahead** with the hedge on your left. Walk on and at the next (tall!) wooden sign, turn **left**.

Climb over the stile and at the waymark sign close to the main road, turn **right** along the footpath. Emerge at Cinder Hill Lane. Cross the main road to The Five Bells.

**MAIN ROUTE** To return to Barcombe from Balneath Manor, walk along the tarmac bridleway through Starvecrow Farm. Where the lane curves, leave it to go through the small metal gate. Walk **straight ahead** across the field. The path runs alongside a lovely wood. Pass the pond, crossing a footbridge. Follow the path ahead along the fence. Cross another footbridge with cattle-ends and **walk onwards**, heading for the fence. Walk up the unsigned grassy path beside the fenced green poultry barn. This is Woodland Farm, an organic egg producer. Reach the track and walk on, following footpath signs **straight ahead** to the road. Cross.

6  **TQ 407 163** Walk **right** for a short distance (25 metres). At the wooden signpost, go **left** across the footbridge and walk along the footpath. It runs alongside the bridleway, Birdshole Lane. Cross several stiles and join the bridleway. Walk on in the same direction. (Be careful at the last stile, where you must turn **right** so that you keep heading in the same direction.) Emerge by Birdshole Cottage and a stony, unmade lane. There's a three-way signpost. Walk **left** towards Sewells Farm along the signed footpath. Walk through the farm and dog agility school. Go through the two gates. Turn **right** across the stile and follow the path back across the next stile and diagonally across the field. Go through the gap in the hedge back to Barcombe Recreation Ground and your car.

# 7 Explore Loxwood Canal

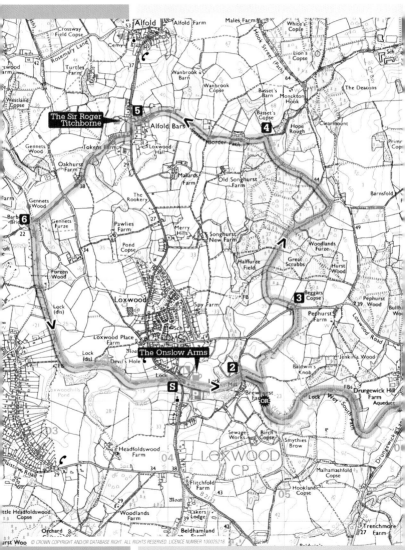

*Walkers at Loxwood Canal*

A tranquil circuit enabling you to enjoy the wildlife of the restored Wey and Arun Canal and the peace of its surrounding woodland and agricultural areas. Drop by one of two noteworthy pubs en route. I also recommend the towpath for a shorter linear walk which is flat and easy for all.

**CREATIVE STARTING POINTS**
- Journeys versus roots
- Reflections
- Flying, floating and sinking
- Earth, air and water

**START** On the towpath by the Wey and Arun Canal Trust 'office'.

**GRID REF** TQ 041 311

**TOTAL ASCENT** 193 ft/59 m

**PARKING** Onslow Arms overflow or Wey and Arun Canal Trust car park (see *www.weyandarun.co.uk* for details).

**PUBLIC TRANSPORT**

*Bus* Try *Compass* travel for bus routes which pass through Loxwood.

**TERRAIN** The tow path is great for easy access. Woodland or field tracks, a few bridleways on hard surfaces. An easy, level walk.

**REFRESHMENTS** The relaxed Onslow Arms in Loxwood, *T* 01403 752 452, does hearty home-cooked food whilst the Sir Roger Tichborne near Alford has beautiful garden views, *T* 01403 751 873. Both are worth a visit.

**OS MAP** Explorer 134: Crawley and Horsham

# 7 Explore Loxwood Canal

*The Wey and Arun Canal Trust* are doing an admirable job in restoring this inland waterway link, which runs all the way from London, via the rivers Wey and Arun, to Littlehampton. Their work will not only make the canal navigable by boat but will also provide a haven for wildlife and a 'wetland corridor' which should help wildlife move between important habitats. Some sections of the towpath are accessible for walks and the restoration project enables many to enjoy this tranquil waterway. They run a variety of boat trips. *www.weyandarun.co.uk*

**Wildlife**

The canal provides a rich variety of habitats for wildlife. In spring, bluebells and wood anemone burst into flower from the shade of the alder and willow trees and the varied vegetation on the banks provides sustenance for a host of abundant dragonflies and damselflies, including the beautiful dainty banded demoiselle. Look out for birds such as herons, great-crested grebes, moorhens, swans and mallards. We managed to spot a kestrel. At dusk, you may glimpse a bat or two – maybe a natterer's bat or a soprano pipistrelle.

**S** TQ 041 311 Walk **east** along the towpath away from the Onslow Arms. Pass a lock.

**2** TQ 046 312

**OPTIONAL ROUTE** For those wanting a short linear easy-access walk – continue **straight ahead** along the towpath for as far as you like before retracing your steps.

**MAIN ROUTE** Walk **left** across the red brick bridge and turn **right** at the public footpath sign to walk along the opposite tow path. At the next (three-way) sign, turn **left** along the footpath. Follow the track around the edge of the field, passing three more signposts. At the fourth signpost, the track leads you into a wood. Follow the footpath **straight ahead**.

**3** TQ 051 317 At the road, go **straight** across and follow the signed footpath past the house. Cross a couple of stiles, a grazing field and then another stile. Follow the track along the fence. At the next signpost, **ignore** the stile and head **straight** on into the woods. Stay on this track. Keep **straight ahead** at the next two signposts and enjoy the flash of butterfly wings and the echo of bird calls in these beautiful woods. Reach a footbridge and follow the signpost **left** along the wide mud track. At the next junction, follow the signed bridleway **straight** on (**ignoring** paths to left and right).Keep **straight ahead** at the next signpost/stile.

**4** TQ 048 331 When you reach the T-junction, turn **left** onto the bridleway. Reach a house and a sign for the *Sussex Border Path*. (You are on it!) Keep walking **straight ahead** until you reach the busy road.

**8.5 km / 5.3 miles**

**5**   **TQ 036 333** Cross the road to visit the Sir Roger Tichborne pub. To continue on the route, turn **left** along the narrow verge and walk along this short road stretch (fast cars!). Turn **right** on Oakhurst Lane, along the Sussex Border Path. When you reach a wooden signpost, turn **left** and leave the lane to follow the Border Path. Go through the gate. Stay on the Border Path, **ignoring** the footpath at the first signpost. Pass another signpost. Reach the woods and continue **straight ahead**, still on the Sussex Border Path and **ignoring** the bridleway leading left. **Ignore** the footpath heading left at next signpost. Pass a small pond.

**6**   **TQ 028 324** Head **left** on the bridleway at the signed crossroads, leaving the Sussex Border Path. Go through a metal gate. You are walking alongside the old canal bed. Pass through another gate. Keep **straight ahead** at the next signpost and stay on the Wey-South footpath along the towpath until you reach the Onslow Arms.

*A female beautiful demoiselle*

*This stretch of the canal, including Southlands Lock, is being rebuilt by the Wey and Arun Canal Trust. Look out for the traditional hedgerow beside the towpath which has been created to provide a valuable wildlife habitat. You will later pass Devil's Hole Lock.*

*Foxglove and oak tree*

# 8 Looping around Time and Science

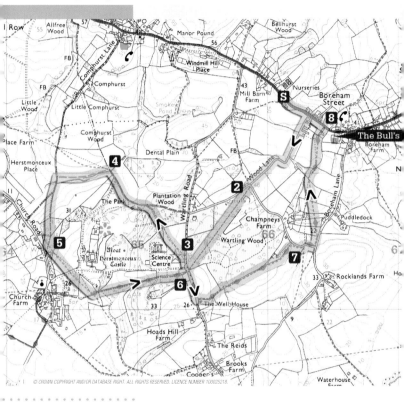

A figure of eight loop through woodland and the grounds of Herstmonceux Castle and Science Observatory with a choice of a traditional pub or tea rooms.

# The Weald

## 7.5 km / 4.6 miles

CREATIVE
STARTING POINTS

• Parallel lines

• Arcs

• Counting time

• Exploration, experiments
  and discovery

*View over the Low Weald*

**START** At car park entrance.
**GRID REF** TQ 661 115
**TOTAL ASCENT** 379 ft/116 m
**PARKING** Wartling Village Hall
car park (gated, so may be locked) or
adjacent lay-by on the A271 between
Herstmonceux and Boreham Street.
**PUBLIC TRANSPORT**
*Bus Stagecoach service* 98 bus
runs through Boreham Street.
*www.stagecoachbus.com*

**TERRAIN** A mix of woodland and
agricultural paths, mainly soft-surfaces.
**REFRESHMENTS** The Bulls Head
pub: welcoming, good food, good ale,
*T* 01323 831 981; Scolfes restaurant
and Tea Rooms, Boreham Street,
*T* 01323 833 296.
**OS MAP** Explorer 124: Hastings
and Bexhill

# 8 Looping around Time and Science

*When early Royal Greenwich Observatory astronomers solved the problem of longitude by establishing 'Greenwich Time', they enabled mariners to chart their position anywhere in the world by using a Greenwich clock or tables in conjunction with studying the position of the stars. Astronomy clearly had practical uses! They then moved on to study the stars and other objects in the sky, to find out what they are and how they work. They later moved to Herstmonceux because London's smoky skies and bright lights were affecting visibility. At Herstmonceux, a team of 'night observers' took photographic shots of specified points in the sky. Exposure time for this precision shot ranged for a single photographic plate from five minutes to an hour or more. Now that's what you call 'shutter-speed'.*

**S**   **TQ 661 115** Cross the A271(!) and turn **right**. Walk along the pavement. After the first bus stop, turn **right** along Wood Lane. Follow it as it snakes along.

**2**   **TQ 658 109** At the junction with Jenners Lane, go **diagonally left** across the stile, following the public footpath through Wartling Wood. Keep to the right of the timber buildings. Walk **straight ahead** past the marker post and metal gate. The path leads you through mixed woodland full of horse chestnut, oak, beech and birch trees. It then runs by a small clearing. Stay on the track until you reach the signpost. Turn **right** at the signpost, following the footpath and passing a small pond. Emerge at the roadside. Turn **right**, passing the entrance to Herstmonceaux Castle and Science Centre.

**3**   **TQ 653 103** Turn **left** at the lay-by just beyond the entrance. Walk through the gate and go **diagonally right** across the field, keeping the Observatory on your left. Cross the stile and walk on along the fence. Cross the footbridge. At the three-way signpost, turn **left**. Walk between two ponds, enjoying the noise of the running water and whispering reeds. The bridlepath runs between fence and hedge, alongside the castle grounds. **Ignore** gates to the side. At the end, go through the gate marked with a yellow arrow.

**4**   **TQ 647 110** At the four-way signpost, turn **left** through the gate to follow the bridleway past the lone oak and onwards across the field. Go through the gate. Turn **left** at the three-way signpost and walk 25 yards along the (muddy?!) farm track.

*Plantation beech wood*

# 8 Looping around Time and Science

*Herstmonceux is a moated castle set in beautiful parkland and Elizabethan gardens. There were significant settlements here before the castle, the earliest of which was mentioned as far back as the Domesday book. In the 12th century, a Saxon lady, Idonea de Herst, married a Norman nobleman, Ingelram de Monceux, and their surnames were combined to give the castle, observatory and village their unusual name. The castle passed into the hands of the Fiennes family who played some significant roles in Tudor times. The house fell into ruin but was rebuilt this century. It is now an International Study Centre.*

*Please note, there is no access to the castle or grounds from the public footpath.*

5 **TQ 643 104** At the next signpost, **veer** left, leaving the track to walk south up the slope. Go through the gate into the woods and walk **straight ahead** past the marker post. At the four-way signpost, go **left** along the footpath, leaving the bridleway. Soon, cross a stile and leave the woods. Walk **straight ahead** across the field. See the Observatory in front of you. Cross the stile and then the castle driveway.

Go **straight ahead** along the footpath and over the stile. Walk **straight ahead** up the field as far as the gate. **Be careful here**, as the inclination is to go the wrong way: you need to turn **left** across the field towards the Observatory. **Ignore** the stile, crossing the footbridge instead. Go through the small metal gate on your right hand side, following the bridleway. Walk up the stony path with occasional steps. Go through the next gate. *This is a section of the 1066 Country Walk.* See the Observatory on your left. Walk **straight ahead**.

Observatory

6  **TQ 653 102** Emerge at the entrance to the Observatory. Rather than retrace your earlier steps, turn **right** along the road to follow the 1066 Country Walk. Go 300 metres along the roadside verge. At a wooden waymarker on the opposite roadside, turn **left** across the stile, still following 1066 Country Walk. Cross the next stile and walk through the trees and **straight up** along the edge of the field. Enjoy views over agricultural land. Keep walking along the field edge, passing a marker post. Pass through the gate.

7  **TQ 661 104** Turn **right** and walk about 100 metres along the lane, (**ignoring** the stile immediately to the right where you join the lane). Turn **left** across the stile signed *Boreham Street*. Follow the 1066 Walk **diagonally right** across the field. Cross the stile in the corner and follow the footpath **straight ahead**. Cross the next stile and walk **diagonally left**. Cross a third stile and walk **straight ahead** once more. Cross yet another stile and walk **diagonally left** and across to the opposite side of the field. Cross and again walk **diagonally left** across the grazing field. Cross the stile near the corner and walk **straight ahead**. Keep walking **straight ahead**, following the marker post and then the signpost. Dramatic sunsets to the left/west for the fortunate. Turn **right** beside the barns across the stile. Walk between the fence and the hedge. Walk down the steps to the busy road.

8  TQ 664 113

OPTIONAL ROUTE Turn **right** to walk into Boreham Street to visit pub/tea rooms.

MAIN ROUTE Turn **left** to return to your car by the village hall.

*The six green domes of Herstmonceux are known as the 'Equatorial Group' and house three reflecting and three refracting telescopes. The copper sheet cladding of the distinctive green domes was designed by Brian O'Rourke to blend into the Sussex Countryside. (It's interesting to compare the design to the recent Amex stadium in our Downland Doddle Walk. Which blends better?) The structure's external walls were clad in knapped flint – a traditional Sussex finish, which was a further attempt by the architect to help the buildings 'blend in'. Unfortunately, astronomers didn't always find the building user-friendly and in 1990, The Royal Greenwich Observatory moved away to Cambridge. This Grade II* listed monument was repaired with National Lottery funds and now alongside the historic telescopes, it houses over 100 very user-friendly interactive hands-on science exhibits.*

# 9 Between Downs and River: Burton Pond

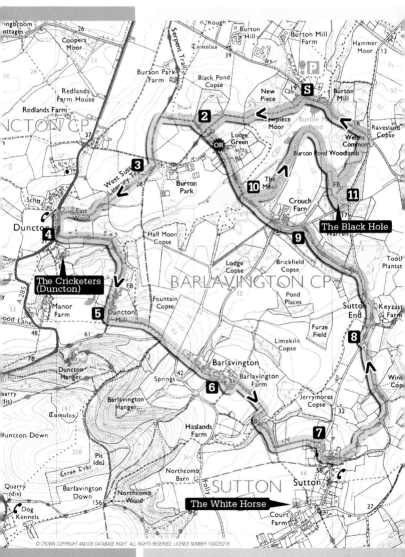

*Swans at Burton Pond*

An interesting walk from a Sussex Wildlife Trust Nature Reserve exploring a peaceful area which offers unexpected views and a choice of two relaxing pubs serving good quality food.

**CREATIVE STARTING POINTS**

- Wild, cultivated, left alone
- Dark and light
- Ripples and grooves
- Wet or dry

**START** At the car park entrance.
**GRID REF** SU 978 180
**TOTAL ASCENT** 466 ft/142 m
**PARKING** Sussex Wildlife Trust car park at Burton Mill, on Burton Park Road between the A285 near Duncton and the B2138 near Watersfield.
**PUBLIC TRANSPORT**
*Train* Stations at Pulborough and Amberley.

**TERRAIN** A complex but rewarding walk. Mainly level, with some hard surfaces and some uneven muddy or boggy sections. Dogs strictly under control in nature reserve.
**REFRESHMENTS**
The Cricketers Freehouse, Duncton *T* 01798 342 473; The White Horse, Sutton, *T* 01798 869 221.
**OS MAP** Explorer 121: Arundel and Pulborough

# 9 Between Downs and River: Burton Pond

*The beginning and end of this walk is tailored to introduce you to the fascinating **Sussex Wildlife Trust Nature Reserve** of Burton Pond. This 16th century hammer pond is both striking and tranquil, fringed with reeds and backed by carr – a wet alder and willow woodland which has evolved over many years, aged trees tumbling to the ground to provide food for wood-loving beetles. Fallen trees also create a break in the canopy so that sunlight can stream through to the woodland floor, enabling sedges and marsh marigolds to flourish.*

**S** SU 978 180 Exit the car park at the Sussex Wildlife Trust sign. **Ignore** the gate opposite. Turn **right** along the road. Cross the bridge and almost immediately, turn **left** along the signed public footpath. Note Burton and Chingford Nature Trail discs. Walk forward a few yards. Go through the gate into the Sussex Wildlife Trust reserve. Walk **straight ahead** on the footpath passing a couple of marker posts and another gate.

Emerge into a clearing. *Look out for the welcoming old sweet chestnut trees on your right, riddled with nest holes. Some may be used by lesser spotted woodpeckers, others by bats. The trees were planted when this land was a part of Burton Park, possibly in the early 18th century.* Walk past the old sweet chestnut trees and go through the gate.

**2** **SU 970 177** Turn **right** through the kissing gate and follow the signposted path.

**OPTIONAL ROUTE** Turn **left** for a short cut to **point 9**.

**MAIN ROUTE** Cross the footbridge. The path curves left, passing Black Pond. **Continue** through the fields. Turn **left** after the stile. Go through the gate, following the public bridleway to Burton Chapel. Turn **right** at the signpost by Burton Chapel.

Walk 15m to the next signpost.

*Burton Park Chapel dates from 1075. It was an important focus for Catholicism from the 17th to the 19th century and the owners provided a priest to say mass there. It's worth a visit as the simply plastered walls and fittings are reminiscent of what many country churches looked like around 1850. The chapel has interesting wall paintings which include a picture of a female saint crucified upside down. Some say this represents Wilqefortis or Uncumber; she grew a beard and was popular with men seeking release from their wives.*

**3** **SU 966 175** Veer **diagonally right** along the footpath, leaving the driveway. Cross the stile. Turn **right** at the signpost, along the public footpath which runs along the tarmac driveway. Turn **left** along the busy road for about 50m.

*Path at Burton Pond Reserve*

# 9 Between Downs and River: Burton Pond

**4** SU 960 170

OPTIONAL ROUTE Walk on a few extra steps to visit to The Cricketers Freehouse.

MAIN ROUTE Turn **left** at Dye House Lane, following the bridleway sign. Walk through Duncton Mill Fishery and some of the way up the hill.

**5** SU 963 164 Turn **left** at the signpost along the bridleway. Before long, views open out over Burton House and the Rother Valley as you walk through the organic dairy farm, Barlavington. Go round the gate and hit the road. **Easy to miss:** immediately turn **left** over a stile hidden in the hedgerow. (**Do not** turn onto the road!) **Walk diagonally** right to climb the next stile. Look for the small arrow on the fence post. Walk **straight ahead**, keeping the fence on your left. Cross the stile, following the yellow footpath arrow. Cross the road and follow the signed footpath **straight ahead**. Cross the footbridge and climb up the path lined with an array of twisted yew trees. Pass through the gate and walk **straight ahead** through Barlavington Farm.

*There are some interesting old graves in this tucked-away, tranquil spot sheltered by the downs.*

**6** SU 971 161 Turn **left** along the lane. At the signpost, follow the footpath **right** through St Mary's Church. Turn **right** past the marker post along the farm track. Keep on this track, passing the three-way signpost. By the last tall barn and marker post, follow the footpath **right**. It opens into a field. Walk **straight ahead**, following the line of the fence. Near the bottom of the slope, look for a stile. Turn **right** and walk about half way along the grazing field. Turn **left** to the stile. Cross stile and footbridge into the woods. Follow the path up to

**11 km / 6.8 miles**

*Water rail*

the **left** into a field. It runs along the edge of the trees. At the signpost, turn left along the footpath. Pass Potcroft house and a marker post. Walk **straight ahead** along the driveway, enjoying marvellous views to your left.

7 **SU 979 156** Turn **right** at the road. Pass St John Baptist Church.

OPTIONAL ROUTE  Continue **straight on** for The White Horse pub.

MAIN ROUTE  After the Old School House, turn **left** along School Lane following the signed footpath. At the end of the houses, follow the signed footpath **straight ahead** onto the grassy track. Cross the stile. Walk **straight ahead** past the next signpost. Cross a field. Cross the next stile and walk **straight on** past the marker post and across another field. Look out for the old signpost under the oak tree and keep walking along the tree-line. Veer **left** at the marker post to next signpost. At the three-way signpost, turn **left** to cross the stile into another field. Cross the next stile, following the signed footpath ahead. *Ground can be wet underfoot.* Walk towards the two oak trees and cross the stile. Follow the signed footpath over two more stiles and on to the road ahead.

8 **SU 982 163** Turn **right** at the road for 300m. Pass the houses. The road becomes more wooded. Turn **left** at the driveway to Sutton End House. Soon, leave the drive-way to follow the bridleway into the trees. This path leads you through the Warren, a developing oak wood-land which is part of the SWT reserve.

# 9 Between Downs and River: Burton Pond

**9** **SU 977 171** At the road, turn **left**. Walk up to Crouch Farm. Where the road bends to the left, leave the road to follow the signed public footpath **straight ahead**. Go through two gates, crossing a farm track to continue on the footpath.

*The reserve also includes a second shallower pond, Chingford, various woodland and wet and dry heath and bogs. Enjoy a quick wander straight ahead to the dam which separates Burton and Chingford Ponds. The muddy edges of Chingford are perfect for visiting migrants such as common and green sandpipers but the pond may eventually be lost if water levels cannot be raised.*

**10** **SU 973 173** This next section is part of the Sussex Wildlife Trust's Nature Trail.

At the signpost before you reach the dam, turn **right** to explore the southern side of the pond. There's a beautiful array of trees to your left. It soon opens out to your right and Burton Pond may be glimpsed through the trees to your left. Keep **straight ahead** at the marker post following the SWT Nature Trail. Watch for sett-holes on the path. The trail runs parallel with the pond edge for a while. *This is one of my favourite parts as the tranche between path and pond is lush with wildlife. The nationally scarce tanner beetle can be found in these woods.* The path follows the line of the fence for a while then runs alongside water. Pass another SWT marker post. *The ground may be boggy underfoot.* Cross a couple of footbridges. Go through a gate and turn **right** to walk along the fence-line. Reach a SWT noticeboard about The Black Hole, *an area with acidic, swampy conditions created by the presence of peat.* Turn **right** through the gate. **Take care** as you cross the boardwalk, here to enable you to enjoy this unusual black water swamp. Follow the SWT trail left as denoted on the marker post. At the road, turn **left**.

*How many tree species can you recognise? The path becomes darker with overhanging canopy as you walk through coniferous woods with western hemlock, western red cedar, sitka spruce and Douglas firs.*

**11** **SU 981 173** At the T-junction, turn **left** towards Byworth. After 150m, reach the marker post and turn **left** through the gate, following the SWT nature trail. Turn right, to walk through Welch's Common. Pass through another gate and walk **straight on**. Walk **right** at the marker post through the gate. Emerge at a road junction. Turn **left** towards Duncton. *As we wandered back to our car, we were lucky enough to hear an owl hoot as a flock of birds were silhouetted against the moonlit pond. A perfect end to the walk.*

*This is dry heathland, home to field crickets, heathers, wavy hair-grass. Look out for the small thornless tree, the alder buckthorn: an important food source for both birds and insects, including the brimstone butterfly.*

Welch's Common

# South Downs

. . . . . . . . . . . . . . . . .

There are few things that can beat the feeling of walking along the top of the Downs. Space, light and the contours of the chalk hills combine to form a unique atmosphere. Breathe deep, feel the chalk underfoot and enjoy the harmony, the varied shades of green. The essence of the Downs is hard to pin down but many 'wild' spaces are becoming increasingly valuable to us as we appreciate the contrast to the busy, urban or technological elements of our lives.

The South Downs are a much-loved feature of our Sussex landscape and their significance in terms of ecology, leisure and history is now recognised through National Park status.

Forever atmospheric and steeped in history, this landscape has shaped the lives of many and continues to do so: farmers, writers, smugglers, men of the cloth, rebels and innovators. It's surprising not just where and what you discover when you're walking, but who. See who you find.

*South Downs Way*

# The South Downs
# – East of Brighton

Our walks in this area share a certain something but it's hard to define. There's an interesting dynamic at play. Imagine that you are walking through a secluded area, tucked away between downland slopes when you follow an ancient droveway round a corner and climb to a ridge-top to discover an expansive vista that cannot fail to please and delight you. Perhaps it's this conflict between flinging your arms out to enjoy open space and the sensation of being enclosed that has caused the area to inspire so many.

A particular mention must go to the area of cliff top downland at Birling Gap. Always spectacular, sometimes windy(!), we explore around and about the cliffs to truly blow away the cobwebs and explore this fascinating area. Don't be put off by the walk being long; it can easily be done in two sections.

*Seven Sisters*

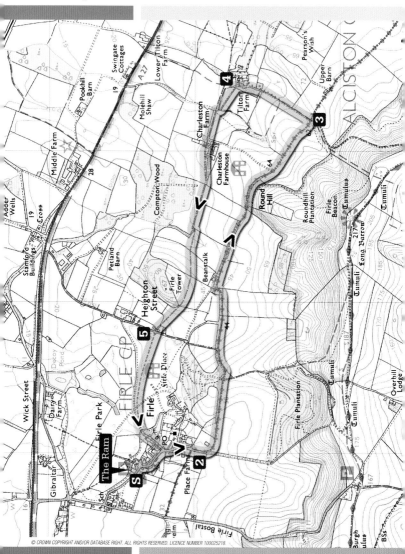

© CROWN COPYRIGHT AND/OR DATABASE RIGHT. ALL RIGHTS RESERVED. LICENCE NUMBER 100025218.

*Downs near Charleston*

Follow in the footsteps of the talented Bloomsbury Set as you wander along an old coach road beneath the pleasing curves of the downs to finish at a traditional country pub. Combine this atmospheric walk with a visit to Charleston during summer months.

**CREATIVE STARTING POINTS**

- Curves and right-angles
- Fertile versus barren
- Discarded, lost or remembered
- Towers, holes and tracks

**START** At the front of the Ram pub.
**GRID REF** TQ 468 074
**TOTAL ASCENT** 346 ft/105 m
**PARKING** Free car park clearly signed on approach to Firle village. It adjoins the Ram. Exit the car park via a white gate in the brick wall and turn right along the footpath to reach the front of the pub.
**PUBLIC TRANSPORT**
*Bus* Service 125 runs between Lewes, Glynde, Firle, Selmeston, Berwick and Alfriston.

**TERRAIN** Paths to Charleston are hard-surfaced but surfaces can be rough and uneven. Paths curve with the downs but most gradients are moderate. Footpaths from Charleston to Firle may be muddy and steep.
**REFRESHMENTS** The Ram in Firle, *T* 01273 858222.
**OS MAP** Explorer 122: Brighton and Hove

# 10 Inspirational Firle and Charleston

*Charleston House was home to Virginia Bell and Duncan Grant. This drew a number of the artists, painters and intellectuals – who became known as the 'Bloomsbury Set' – to the area. Whilst their talent was extraordinary, their lifestyles and sometimes complicated relationships have also attracted discussion. Today, the ideas, theories, literature and art which they left behind them remain internationally appreciated and discussed. Regular visitors included writer Virginia Woolf, economist Keynes, TS Eliot, Lytton Strachey and EM Forster. The house has long been recognised as a creative hub but how did the landscape affect their thoughts? It's worth considering as you enjoy your walk!*

*Bloomsbury Set members who feature around Charleston:*
*Vanessa Bell 1879-1961 painter, married to Duncan Bell and later, lived with Duncan Grant.*
*Arthur Clive Heward Bell 1881-1964, art critic and author.*
*Duncan Grant 1885-1978, painter, lived with Vanessa Bell from 1914.*
*John Maynard Keynes 1883-1946, economist, university lecturer, senior civil servant.*
*Lydia Lopokova, 1892-1981, dancer with Diaghilev's Ballet Russes.*
*Virginia Woolf, 1882-1941, author, essayist, publisher.*

**S** TQ **468 074** Start at the front of the pub. Walk **straight ahead** towards Firle Stores, The Shire House and St Peters Church, following the sign. *Notice Talland House, one of a pair of Edwardian semi-detached villas. Virginia named it 'Little Talland House' when she rented the villa in 1911.*

Divert **left** along the narrow footpath to explore the church. *Vanessa Bell and Duncan Grant are buried in a corner of the graveyard.* **Continue** up the lane, passing Shire House.

**2** TQ **470 070** Walk **straight ahead** following the wooden waymark-signed bridleway. Follow the track round past the red-arrowed marker. Walk up the chalky track with views to the downs on your right and the flint wall on your left. At the top of the slope, go **straight on** following the red arrow on the marker post. The track becomes more wooded. Pass the bridleway going left. Keep walking.

Pass the private road. See Firle Tower on your left. Soon pass a barn. Keep walking **straight ahead** on this roughly-surfaced track. *The downs to your right have a pleasing curve; the track falls and rises to the rhythmic pattern of your footsteps and views open up to your left, further adding to the feeling of space. Walking along this old coach road gives you a sense of following a well-trodden and somehow timeless path.* The path rises again. Pass distant barns on your left and a scrubby bank rises up right.

**3** TQ **492 062** Walk **left** along the stony bridleway by the signed marker post, leaving the old coach road/byway. Pass the house, 'Tilton Meadow' and soon some barns.

**4**  **TQ 494 067** Reach a sign/gate to Tilton House. Follow the signed bridleway **left** past the marker post. You are on Firle Estate. Turn **left** towards Charleston along the drive. Go over the cattle grid. Pass a pond on your right and see Charleston House.

Walk on past Charleston buildings and WC. Go **straight ahead** through the gate to follow the bridleway. Almost immediately walk through a second gate. Go on through the wooden gate and walk towards Firle Tower through the field.

*Tilton House is where economist Keynes lived with his lover, the Russian ballerina, Lopokova.*

*St Peters Church*

# 10 Inspirational Firle and Charleston

*Vanessa Bell, Duncan Grant and Bunny (David Garnett) lived at Charleston (Charleston) House from 1916 to 1919. Duncan and Bunny had been told to find work when seeking exemption from military service and they hoped to find agricultural work in the area. The interior of Charleston House was painted by the artists Duncan Grant and Vanessa Bell and is well worth seeing. Both house and gardens are open to visitors between April and October but do close for winter. See **www.charleston.org.uk** for further information.*

*Firle Tower is a Grade II listed building, built by the third Viscount Gage in 1819 as a rather unusual three-storey circular game-keepers cottage. He placed it at the top of a small hill so that the game-keeper could signal to the keeper of Plashet deer-park at Ringmer, which he also owned.*

*Firle House and restaurant is open to the public during the summer on selected days: see **www.firle.com** for further information.*

At the marker post, go **left** through the gateway.

Head for the small gate in the far hedge boundary. Go through the gate and walk across or around the field to the wooden waymarker sign. Go through the open gate and head up and across the field to the gap in the border opposite.

Walk across the track to Firle Estate. Go **straight ahead**, following the bridleway signed on the marker post. A short stretch of narrow track opens out into a field. A narrow mud track snakes down and across the field. It leads to some houses. Go through a metal gate, along a small driveway and through some gateposts.

**5** TQ 478 072 Cross the lane/bridleway. Walk **straight ahead** through the gate and follow the footpath across Firle Park *(Note: this footpath may be diverted if horse-jumping trials are in session.)*

Head towards the stony track, passing some way in front of Firle House. Cross the tarmac driveway and continue **straight ahead** along the stony track. Follow the footpath through the kissing gate to leave Firle Estate. Walk along the walled lane. Emerge by Firle Stores and turn **right** to return to the pub and car park.

*For more information, read 'The Bloomsbury Trail in Sussex', Judy Moore, S.B. Publications, 1996 or visit Charleston House.*

*Rupert Brooke and Virginia sat in Firle Park one Sunday morning to write poetry. I can only speculate what their words were but would be interested to see the park through their eyes. Originally built in Tudor times by the Gage family, who still live there today, the house boasts two art collections: the Cowper Collection, which includes Dutch paintings such as a group portrait by Van Dyke, and the Grenfell Collection – a mix of furniture and paintings.*

*Downs near Charleston*

# 11 Mysterious Guardian of the Downs

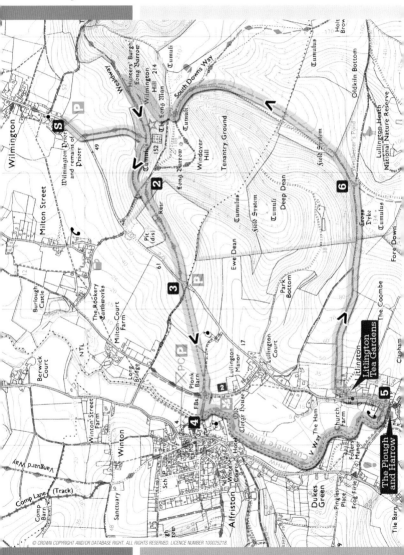

*Chalk path near Wilmington*

A stunning downland walk which begins at landscape mystery, the Long Man. You are treated to exhilarating views followed by an easy stretch down through crop fields and along the banks of the River Cuckmere to Litlington, where you may choose to eat at either pub or tea rooms. A dramatic climb up to Winchester's Pond on the edge of Lullington Heath allows you to return along the ridge to the Long Man.

### CREATIVE STARTING POINTS

- Symbols and figures
- chalk, soil and growth
- Movement versus stillness
- Rebellion, appeasement and solidarity

**START** Long Man and Priory car park, Wilmington.

**GRID REF** TQ 543 042

**TOTAL ASCENT** 1036 ft/316 m

**PARKING** Long Man and Priory car park, Wilmington WC (signed Litlington). Alternative parking further along the road at **point 3**.

**PUBLIC TRANSPORT**

*Train* British Rail stations at Berwick (3 miles) and Polegate (2.5 miles).

**TERRAIN** Downland and river bank paths. Some climbing.

**REFRESHMENTS** Plough and Harrow, Litlington, *T* 01323 870632; Litlington Tea Gardens, *T* 01323 870222; Giant's Rest, Wilmington, *T* 01323 870207.

**OS MAP** Explorer 123: Eastbourne and Beachy Head

# 11 Mysterious Guardian of the Downs

*'The Giant keeps his secret and from his hillside flings out a perpetual challenge.'*
Rev. A. A. Evans

*The Long Man has baffled historians and archeologists for many years. Is it a fertility symbol? An ancient Warrior? An early 18th century folly? Known pictures date back to 1710 when it was probably only visible in certain light conditions. Some think it dates back as far as the Iron Age. Others think it's the work of an artistic monk, whilst certain Roman coins bear a similar figure. More recently, it's been camouflaged and painted green in World War Two, reinforced with bricks, vandalised with an added 20-foot phallus and 'adapted' to female form by ITV show Trinny and Susannah. The Long Man Morris Men dance there every May Day at dawn and it's the site of various neo-pagan ceremonies. The Long Man is many things to many people!*

**S** TQ 543 042 Exit the car park, cross the lane and follow the footpath to the Long Man. *One of the best views of him is as you approach.* Go through the gate and turn immediately **right**, passing the Long Man and dew pond. Walk along the fence. See Arlington Reservoir on your right. A chalky path becomes apparent as you climb. You may see Firle Beacon on your distant right. At the top go through a gate and turn **left** to walk up the slope, following the bridleway.

**2** TQ 538 035 Turn **right** onto the chalky downhill track. This is the South Downs Way (SDW) but it's not signed. *The views here are something special. See Alfriston ahead as you descend.* Go through the gate.

**3**  TQ 532 032 Cross the road, *(see the alternative car park on your left)* continuing on the SDW for 100m. Look for a partially obscured stile and turn **left**, heading diagonally across two crop fields towards Alfriston church spire. Go through the gap in the trees and turn **right** along the narrow track. Emerge by a gate to Great Meadow Barn. Walk **left** along the path and out through the gate. Walk **right** along the road and, almost immediately turn **left** opposite Great Meadow Barn. Walk along the bridleway, keeping **straight ahead** at the first signpost. Cross the first small footbridge.

*Look out for the distant Litlington horse, a chalk figure which was cut in 1924. Local men cut the horse overnight with a full moon to see by, hoping to startle the locals with the sudden appearance of the horse in the morning. An earlier horse was rumoured to either be in commemoration of Queen Victoria's coronation or a youthful prank. The National Trust now own the land at Frog Firle.*

*The Long Man*

# 11 Mysterious Guardian of the Downs

*Lullington Heath is a fine example of chalk heath. This unique habitat enables a mixture of chalk-loving plants to grow alongside plants that need acid soils. At Lullington Heath, the acid soil is as deep as 20cm in some places, enabling acid-loving species such as heather, bell-heather and tormentii to grow among chalk-loving plants such as thyme, salad burnet and dropwort.*

*How is a chalk heath made? During the last Ice Age, winds eroded and carried sand and dust from the glacier-fronts of the Northern Ice Sheet. This sand and dust was blown south and then dropped – leaving acid soil on chalk bedrock. Over time, human activity such as ploughing can mix together the pockets of acid and calcareous soil. Little of the original chalk heath survives today and this is the largest remaining area in the South Downs. Chalk heath covers just under a third of the Reserve and free-range goats help maintain the heath through grazing. Elsewhere, bushes, chalk grassland and valley grassland form a patchwork across the site. This is a fabulous place to see lots of butterflies, including common species such as red admiral and browns. You may see rarer species such as silver-spotted skipper, adonis blue, grayling and the chalkhill blue.*

**4** TQ 522 031 Turn **left**, following the SDW towards Exceat just before the white footbridge. Walk along the banks of the River Cuckmere for nearly 2 km. See Litlington church spire on your left and go through a kissing gate. Walk **right** along the river. Keep **left** at the first post. Turn **left** along Vanguard Way at the second post.

**5** TQ 523 017

**OPTIONAL ROUTE** At the road in Litlington, turn **right** for the Plough and Harrow.

**MAIN ROUTE** To continue on our walk, turn **left**, passing Litlington Tea Gardens and walk along the road. Pass St Michael Church. Turn **right** at flint Church Farm, along the bridle-way. Immediately head **left** at the marker post up the long steep flint track. The path levels out towards the top and there are fantastic views back over the downs.

At the marker post, continue **straight ahead** up the slope. Pass a stile.

**6** TQ 539 019 At the noticeboard for Lullington Heath, turn **left**. Look at Winchester's Pond. Go through the gateposts. Go through the gate following the bridleway towards the ridge ahead. Fantastic views to sea on left. **Walk on.** Continue **straight ahead** at the signpost. **Easy to confuse:** at the end of the field, **ignore** the gate straight ahead and stile in the corner. Instead, just before exiting the field, Walk **right** towards Arlington Reservoir and through the gate to follow the bridleway/ Wealden Way **straight ahead** back down. Turn **left** at the marker post to walk back past the Long Man and **right** to the car park.

*Lullington Heath*

Cliffs at Seven Sisters

A beautiful walk taking you through secluded Crowlink with its 'artist's light', along a section of the classic Seven Sisters cliff top trail to Birling Gap and then veering around Friston on lesser-known paths to climb Willingdon Hill. Finally, drop by the welcoming Eight Bells at Jevington before returning through Friston Forest.

The walk can easily be split into two shorter walks north and south of the A259.

**START** At the far end of the National Trust car park at Crowlink.
**GRID REF** TV 548 977
**TOTAL ASCENT** 1780 ft/543 m
**PARKING** Crowlink National Trust car park (charge payable), Crowlink Lane. Turn off the A259 at Friston Church.
**PUBLIC TRANSPORT**
*Bus* For Birling Gap: 13X bus, Brighton to Eastbourne (via Seaford), Sundays all year and daily during the summer. For Crowlink: 12A and 12B bus or 13X, Brighton to Eastbourne (via Seaford). See Brighton and Hove Bus and Coach Company for timetables between Brighton and Eastbourne.

*Train* stations at Eastbourne and Seaford.
**TERRAIN** A good amount of climbing and some rough ground mix with some easier paths and descents. Stunning views. **Stay away from cliff edges** – erosion or poor weather can be fatal. Navigation in Friston Forest can be tricky.
**REFRESHMENTS** National Trust cafe and bar at Birling Gap; The Tiger Inn in East Dean, *T* 01323 423 209; The Eight Bells in Jevington, *T* 01323 484 442; Jevington Tea Garden (seasonal), *T* 01323 489 692.
**OS MAP** Explorer 123: Eastbourne and Beachy Head

© CROWN COPYRIGHT AND/OR DATABASE RIGHT. ALL RIGHTS RESERVED. LICENCE NUMBER 100025218.

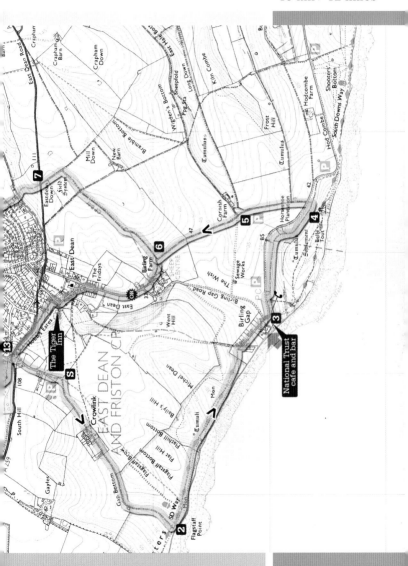

# 12 Coast, Wilderness and Forest

Crowlink was once known as a famous cart gap, providing easy access to the sea. East Sussex smuggling gangs from places such as Alfriston and Jevington were quick to spot the area's potential and contraband would have been hauled through Crowlink from beached ships. It even gave rise to the name 'Genuine Crowlink' which, chalked on the side of a gin barrel, was the guarantee of a good drink. (For more detailed information, see www.smuggling.co.uk.)

**S** **TV 548 977** Go through the gate and follow the tarmac bridleway as it curves right through Crowlink. Follow the track alongside the flint wall as it runs down towards the sea. Go through a gate at the cattle grid and pass through some houses. Keep walking. Go through another gate and walk on, following the line of the fence. Go through another gate. **Walk on**, passing the dew pond, towards the sea. *This is an old smugglers path.*

**2** **TV 537 968** At the cliff edge, turn **left**. Climb the 'sister' to the viewpoint where there's a handy bench.

Climb the next two sisters, passing a war memorial. See the distant red-roofed barn on your left. See Birling Gap below. Walk through a gate, along the path and through another gate. Turn **right** along the flinty path and down to Birling Gap.

**3** TV 554 960

**OPTIONAL ROUTE** Turn **right** to visit Birling Gap with its coastguard cottages, cliff-top cafe, bar, shingle beach and WC.

**MAIN ROUTE** Continue **straight on**. At Birling Gap Road, turn **right** into Birling Gap car park, then turn **left** into the extra section of the car park. Join the path by the bus stop. **Walk along**, staying roughly parallel (15/20m distance) with the road. **Walk on** through the small copse. A couple of hundred metres after you emerge, look for the distant signpost on the far side of the road.

**4** **TV 563 956** Turn **left** towards the signpost. Cross the road and walk along the bridleway towards East Dean Down through Cornish Farm. *Look behind you to see Belle Tout lighthouse. Rumour has it that King George VI and his wife Lady Elizabeth Bowes-Lyon used to holiday at the lighthouse in the early thirties.*

**5** **TV 563 962 Easy to Miss:** Where the concrete bridleway curves right towards Cornish Farm barns, **leave the path** to veer **left** along the fence. Go towards and through two small gates. **Keep walking** along the fence. Go through the gate, walking along the ancient sunken track beside the flint wall.

**6** **TV 559 969** By the corner of the flint wall at the end of the field:

**SHORT CUT** To head home via the Tiger pub, go **left**, walk behind the sheep centre and turn **right** along Birling Gap Road. At East Dean, turn **left** along the minor road to find the Tiger Inn. **Walk past** the front of the pub to where the road meets a slightly bigger road at right angles. **Cross the road** and **follow** the footpath opposite. It runs along the A259 and back to Friston Church and your car park.

**MAIN ROUTE** Turn **right** at the marker post. Climb the grassy path through the grazing field. **Ignore** the first gate, continuing **straight ahead**. The path is not always clear. Go through the gate at the far end of the field. Turn **left**, following the bridleway signed A259 (not suitable for horses). Go through the gate. Cross the busy(!) road.

*Take care near cliff edges!*
*Seven Sisters is a dynamic landscape where the sea, the light and the land interact. The chalk cliffs at Birling Gap are eroding by up to a metre a year, with cracks evident along the cliff top. The coastal strip is chalk grassland, evolved through centuries of grazing and management. This nationally rare habitat is valued for its ability to support as many as 50 different species of plants and grasses within a single square metre. Look out for downland plants such as milkwort, wild thyme, cowslip, dropwort and bird's foot trefoil and butterflies such as adonis blue, dark green fritillary or chalkhill blue. An ever-changing landscape, it inspires us with its strength, its vulnerability and its ability to adapt.*

Red admiral

## 12 Coast, Wilderness and Forest

**7** **TV 565 980** Climb the stile and follow the signed footpath **right** along the opposite fence. Walk to the **left** through the gate. Turn **right** along the grassy path towards the wooden signpost. Turn **left** along the permissive signed bridleway towards Willingdon Hill. Go through the small gate and follow the line of the fence. At the multi-directional signpost by the stile, head **diagonally left** along the bridleway to Willingdon Hill. *Houses share your beautiful views over Eastbourne downland. This is one tough hill: let the views distract you!*

As the houses run out, before the aerial pole, go **left** through the gate and onwards. **Walk up** the hill, passing the aerial pole and following the signed but not obvious grassy track. It follows the fence. *Look out for ridge top views back over a vast swathe of downland, the distant sea, and forwards, towards the course of your remaining walk in Friston Forest.*

Crowlink

**8** **TV 564 995** Go through the gate and turn **right** to reach the peak of Willingdon Hill. At the dilapidated marker post, turn **left** along the unclear grassy track to the clump of trees: Willingdon Hill. At the signpost, walk **straight ahead** through the gate towards Butts Brow car park. Walk **straight on** past the clump of trees. Views open up over the low Weald. Pass through a gate and return to the lower footpath, passing the stone way-marker. Go through a gate.

**9** **TQ 576 009** Turn **left** at the chalk and flint path and marker post. Follow the track towards Jevington. **Walk along** the old cobbled path through the copse. **Ignore** the stile. The path turns into a road. Arriving in Jevington, turn **right at** the T-junction with the main road. Almost immediately, turn **left** up Church Lane along the South Downs Way by the flint wall.

**10** **TQ 561 015** At St Andrews Church:

**OPTIONAL ROUTE** For a 400-metre diversion to the pub, turn **right** to follow the path round St Andrews church. Go through the swing gate. Follow the footpath along the flint wall and the road to the welcoming Eight Bells. The pub boasts lovely views from the garden, is open all day, serves food until 3pm. *www.8bellsonline*

**MAIN ROUTE** **Walk on** past the pub on the chalk bridle-way (South Downs Way) towards Alfriston. There's a bit of a climb! Turn **left** along the bridleway at the signpost. Ascend gradually on the wooded path. Go through the gate and walk **straight ahead** along the open path. Go through the gate and walk **straight on** towards the marker post. Veer **left**, along the bridleway.

# 12 Coast, Wilderness and Forest

*St Mary the Virgin Friston Parish Church is small but well worth a wander. The churchyard gate is known as a Tapsell gate, an unusual design which is thought to be unique to Sussex churches. The oldest part – the nave – could date back as far as Edward the Confessor's reign, around 1042. The interior is lovely with a monument to Thomas Selwyn (d.1613), his wife and their six daughters. The churchyard is interesting. Look for the grave of Thomas Fletcher, an excise man, who, in 1750, was pushed to his death by smugglers over a cliff edge. There is also a wooden cross carved with the legend 'WASHED ASHORE' beneath which many bodies tragically washed ashore at Birling Gap are said to be buried.*

**11** TQ 554 009 At the bench and marker post, turn **right** into Friston Forest along the bridleway. Turn **left** along the chalk track at the first crossroads (unsigned). Stay on this track for some time, **ignoring** all offshoots. The path curves south and there's a fork: keep **left**, staying on your track. Cross a bridleway to Friston (small marker post) and several green family cycling trail signs.

**12** TV 538 989 At the large crossroads with the tall red and white stripey posts, turn **left**. **Veer left** at the fork. See the water mains building on your right. **Walk round** the metal barrier. Turn **right** at the flint wall and follow the footpath. Pass a house. **Follow** the path as it narrows and heads into the woods. Hit a T-junction of paths and, where the flint wall ends, turn **left**. At the telegraph poles, follow the track right into the woods. When the track climbs, you know that you are nearly at Friston. And believe me, at the end of a walk, it's quite a climb. Watch out for protruding metal pole-ends. Walk **straight ahead** through the gate.

**13** TV 551 982 Cross busy Friston junction(!) and turn **right** along Crowlink Lane, passing Friston Church and pond. Continue back to your car.

*Walking on the Downs*

# The South Downs – Central

One of the things which makes the South Downs unusual as a national park is its accessibility. This is particularly the case for the walks in this central section, several can be quickly reached from local stations.

It never ceases to amaze me how easy it is to get into from the cities into an area of downland with such a true 'National Park' feel. A landscape steeped in history, disguised by seasonal and temporal changes and always unpredictable. Clouds, wind, people, animals, birds: you never quite know what you are going to see. A landscape whose wildness feels even more precious when viewed against the distant roofscape of Brighton. And that's the brilliant thing about the Downs, they're there, so near, and yet…

Field scabious by chalk path

# 13 Wolstonbury: A Significant Hill

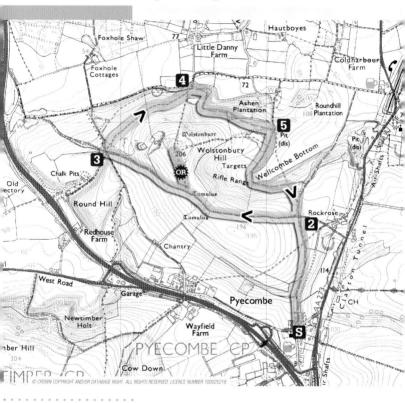

This varied walk leads you around Wolstonbury, a hill of historic and environmental significance. It features far-reaching views, open downs and woodland with just one noticeable climb.

*Common-spotted orchid on chalk grassland at Wolstonbury Hill*

**CREATIVE STARTING POINTS**

- Up, down and balance
- Rough, tough, delicate
- Secret versus flamboyant
- Survival, adaptability and surrender

**START** The crossroads between Church Hill and Church Lane in the centre of Pyecombe between the A23 and the A273. Church Lane is the road beside The Plough.

**GRID REF** TQ 292 126

**TOTAL ASCENT** 670 ft/200 m

**PARKING** Small car park by play area in The Wyshe or roadside by crossroads.

**PUBLIC TRANSPORT**

*Bus* Regular bus routes from Brighton/ Haywards Heath to Pyecombe.

*Train* The nearest train station is Hassocks.

**TERRAIN** Mud or chalk tracks. High start means great views. One noticeable climb. Uneven underfoot on footpath across Wolstonbury.

**REFRESHMENTS** The Plough in Pyecombe, *T* 01273 842 796.

**OS MAP** Explorer 122: Brighton and Hove

# 13 Wolstonbury: A Significant Hill

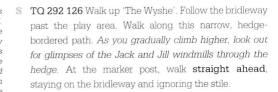

*Wolstonbury Hill includes an area of chalk grassland. This particularly diverse habitat can support as many as 50 separate plant species in a single square metre as well as any associated animal species. Eleven species of orchids are found here, including the rare man orchid.*

*Also look out for the adonis blue, a rare butterfly which enjoys a symbiotic relationship with the ant colonies here. The butterfly chrysalis is protected by the ants. Why? Once it's a caterpillar, they milk the sweet sugary honeydew from the caterpillar's poisonous gland, offering continuing protection to the growing caterpillars from predatory wasps. The managed grazing on Wolstonbury enables the ant hills to survive. Somehow those ant hills don't look quite the same once you know about their role!*

*Pyramidal orchid
Photo: Kieron Huston*

**S**  **TQ 292 126** Walk up 'The Wyshe'. Follow the bridleway past the play area. Walk along this narrow, hedge-bordered path. *As you gradually climb higher, look out for glimpses of the Jack and Jill windmills through the hedge.* At the marker post, walk **straight ahead**, staying on the bridleway and ignoring the stile.

**2**  **TQ 292 133** The path opens into a crossroads. Walk past the marker post and turn **left**, following the bridleway through the gate onto the National Trust access land of Wolstonbury Hill. Follow the path straight ahead.

*Views to the right over Hurstpierpoint and Hassocks are far-reaching. Look behind you to see one of my favourite views of the Jack and Jill windmills.*

At the top of the slope, go through a gate to follow the track **straight ahead** between two fences. *Views to the left over Newtimber Hill, with the line of the downs beyond.* Pass a step-over stile.

**OPTIONAL ROUTE** Take the path heading **right** if you wish to expore the 'fort' at Wolstonbury.

It's probably easiest to retrace your steps to pick up our route by the step-over stile as the later directions can be easy to miss.

**MAIN ROUTE** Walk **straight ahead** on the chalk bridle-way. Go through the gate and stay on the chalk bridle-way. *Sadly the A23 is clearly audible. You may also hear the splutter and ratchet of machinery at the nearby chalk pits.* Walk down, passing the three rounded basins of Wolstonbury on your right and the copse on your left.

3  TQ 279 138 This next turn is **easy to miss**: where the path divides you will see one track goes left to a gate (not initially visible) in the copse, one goes straight ahead down the hill and if you look to the right, there's a marker post and a grassy not-so-obvious footpath. Turn **right** along this grassy track, passing the marker post.

Keep **straight ahead** on this track. See Danny House down to your left.

*I was recently lucky enough to hold a 3000-year old axe-head which was found on the hill – an experience that puts time into perspective! The edge of the axe-head was a perfect line. Perhaps its use was ceremonial? The fort at Wolstonbury is unusual for a bronze-age enclosure in that the ditch is inside the ramparts, leading some to speculate that it was built with peace in mind.*
*If you'd like to find out more about the fascinating history and ecology of Wolstonbury, why not go on a guided walk with knowledgeable National Trust staff (**www.nationaltrust.org.uk/devils-dyke**) or join Friends of Wolstonbury* ***www.wolstonbury.com***

*View from Wolstonbury Hill*

# 13 Wolstonbury: A Significant Hill

*Towards the end of the First World War, Lloyd George stayed at Danny House. He walked on Wolstonbury Hill with Smuts and Borden and is even rumoured to have prompted a security scare by misplacing secret papers during a walk – perhaps the views distracted him! It was at Danny House on 13th October 1918 that the terms of the Armistice to be offered to Germany were agreed.*

Cross the stile and follow the narrow track. The path leads into a copse (slippery and uneven, steep ground underfoot). **Keep walking** in the same direction. Come through the trees to where the narrow path forks. Take the **left fork**, walking slightly downwards along the line of and then back into the woods. Cross the stile and join the bridleway, turning **right** so that you keep walking in the same direction.

4   **TQ 284 142** At the marker post in the clearing, turn **right** following the bridleway up into the woods. The path bends and then climbs steadily upwards until you reach a gate. *See the Jack and Jill windmills in the distance ahead.* Follow the bridleway **straight ahead** to the gate. Go through.

5   **TQ 290 139** At the bridleway sign, turn **right**. **Ignore** a stile on your right. Pass a fenced dewpond. This is Wellcombe Bottom. *Wolstonbury was used for rifle-shooting training during WW2 and perhaps even further back, according to old maps. Target gear has been found in this area.* The steep slopes of the downs are all around you. Go through the gate and follow the chalky track **left** and then upwards. This is the steepest climb of the walk. As you emerge onto open downland, you should recognise the view of Wolstonbury to your right. **Ignore** the stiles and return to the top corner of the field and through the gate which you will recognise from earlier. Turn **right** at the crossroads and follow the familiar bridleway back to Pyecombe.

*View from Wolstonbury Hill*

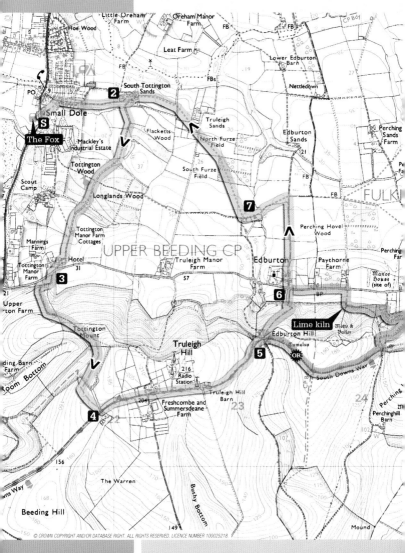

*South Downs Way*

An exhilarating mix of downland, agricultural Sussex and wild woodland. One very steep climb up Tottington Mount to the South Downs Way and a descent from Edburton Hill. Wonderful views through much of the walk.

### CREATIVE STARTING POINTS

- Tools, transport, transformation
- Man, woman, land and sea
- Urban versus rural
- Forwards, backwards

**START** Footpath opposite The Fox pub in Small Dole.

**GRID REF** TQ 214 127

**TOTAL ASCENT** 727 ft/222 m

**PARKING** Henfield Road in Small Dole. Look out for the Tottington Wood brown sign to enter the free car park at the village hall (TQ 212 121) or park at The Fox if you're going to eat there – just let the proprietor know.

**PUBLIC TRANSPORT**

*Bus* Holmbush Centre free bus from Burgess Hill station to Shoreham via Small Dole.

See *www.compass-travel.co.uk*

**TERRAIN** A real mix of woodland, agricultural footpaths and downland grass and chalk. Steep in places.

**REFRESHMENTS** Friendly, down-to-earth atmosphere and reasonably priced food at The Fox in Small Dole, *T* 01273 491 196. There's also a bar menu at Tottington Manor, *T* 01903 815 757.

**OS MAP** Explorer 122: Brighton and Hove

## 14 Tottington: Downland, Farmland & Wood

**S** **TQ 214 127** Look for the green-signed footpath opposite The Fox pub. Walk **between** a fence and some flats. At the wooden waymarker, walk **left** past the goal post towards the house. At the next signpost, **walk on** into the copse and across the footbridge following the footpath. Turn **right** along the lane. Keep following the public footpath on towards Sands Farm.

**2** **TQ 221 128** At the green metal barn, turn **right** following the signpost to double-back on yourself before heading for the trees. Go through the gate and walk **straight on** through the field. Cross the next stile and follow the footpath through privately owned Tottington and Longlands Woods. The narrow, possibly overgrown, path soon widens. Walk **straight ahead** at the signpost, following this track on through the woods. *This woodland is teeming with wildlife: a variety of bird calls, rabbits, butterflies, grey squirrels and foxes may be evident if you're lucky.*

Leave the wood and go through the gate. Follow the signed footpath straight ahead. After the track curves, and before you reach the barn, look for the waymarker sign. Walk **left** along the fence. Follow the footpath **right**.

*Detour left along the lane and back into Tottington Manor next door for refreshments. There's a terrace with great views.*

**3** **TQ 215 115** Turn **right** along the lane. Pass farm buildings. Turn **left** towards the downs up the bridleway (wooden sign may be obscured under foliage). The pleasant path becomes more open as it climbs. It soon climbs steeply but you are rewarded by the views. Pass through a gate. Head **left** along the grassy track. Keep climbing Tottington Mount until you reach the marker post. Be careful navigating hereabouts – there are no signs! You must go **right** here, along the grassy track.

Pass another marker post. At the second marker post, head **left** up between the fences. See the sea to your right. Go through the gate.

4   TQ 219 104 Walk **left** on the South Downs Way (SDW), here an unmade road. *This is a beautiful area of the downs where I challenge you not to uplifted by the dip, curve and swell of the land, the song of the larks or the lemon-scent of the crops.* Pass the youth hostel, grazing fields and Truleigh House. At the sign post, keep **straight ahead** on this easy stretch of the SDW with magnificent sea views over and beyond Brighton. Pass the pylon and buildings. Head on down the chalky track. Pass the National Trust sign for Fulking Escarpment. See the mound to your left which is home to several scrubby trees, a bench and two overgrown headstones. *By the tree, there are a couple of marked graves.* Stay on the SDW until you reach the gate and a four-way sign post.

*A 'bostal' is a Sussex word for a track up the side of a steep hill. It is one of the more commonly recognised examples of Sussex dialect today due, perhaps, to its inclusion on maps. There's an interesting piece in Robert Macfarlane's book, 'Wild Places', which considers the current dominance of road atlases and GPS and how this could affect our awareness of natural landscape features. Observing rivers and forests and contours on maps and having words to describe specific landscape features can only widen what we see.*

*Chalk track*

**5** TQ 232 110 Here leave the SDW. **Do not** cross the stile. Walk **left** through the gate onto the unsigned bridleway. Soon, pass a marker post by the tree. Walk on down. *It's very steep and could be slippery but feels wilder then more established paths. The northern slopes of the Downs here support many butterflies such as the marbled white and six-spot burnett moth. You may also see fragrant and pyramidal orchids.* Towards the bottom, the path leads you through a copse. Walk **left** at the marker post, doubling back past the post and along the fence. At the signpost, follow the bridleway **right** through the gate.

*A combe is a short valley or hollow on a hillside, such as a chalk escarpment and the downland contours hereabouts would provide plenty of places to hide.*

**OPTIONAL EXTENSION** History enthusiasts may want to continue along the SDW and then drop down the bostal track from Perching Hill.

At the four-way signpost, cross the stile and **walk up the slope** with the fence on your right. Pass a stile and follow the gradually descending mud and chalk SDW track. Reach a dip with a pylon where paths cross. (The site of the mediaeval village of Perching is off to the right on a permissive bridleway.) Turn **left**, following the yellow arrow on the marker post to descend to the left of the pylon, on the chalk bostal track. See Fulking village in the distance below you. Paths soon merge between three mounds at the signpost. Follow the wide chalk track as it curves left away from Fulking.

*Lime kilns were used to burn chalk with charcoal to create lime, which was mainly used for improving clay fields or in the building industry. Today, you can see the brick face where the lime was removed and, behind that, the bottle-shaped hole which was the kiln. The kiln was loaded with layers of chalk from the quarry behind it and with charcoal, probably from Furze Field woods (see **point 7**), north of Edburton. The kiln worked continuously: as lime was removed below more chalk and charcoal was added at the top.*

Look out for the historic flint and brick lime kiln on your left, embedded into the escarpment and safeguarded by National Trust ownership.

The path is joined by a footpath and levels out. Walk **straight ahead**, past the marker post and on through the gate, leaving Fulking Escarpment. Turn **left** for an unavoidable stretch along the roadside. Just after you

enter Edburton, look out for the postbox at Aburton Farmhouse opposite the bridleway sign. Rejoin the main route at **point 6**.

**6**  TQ 234 113

**MAIN ROUTE**  Cross the road to the postbox and follow the bridleway sign through the farm house gate. Walk along the walled, then fenced, then hedged track. **Ignore** the first possible crossroads/gaps in the hedge that you reach.

In sight of the four-way wooden signpost, walk **left** along the footpath with the hedge on your left. Follow the footpath into the copse and cross the footbridge. **Walk on** along the fenced garden following the footpath sign.

**7**  **TQ 230 119** At the four-way marker post by the foot-bridge, head **right**, along the fence. Follow the track around the edge of the field, turning **left** at the corner to walk beside the trees. At the signpost/wooden fencing, head **right** across the small footbridge. Walk **straight through** the Furze Field Woods, *the possible source of charcoal for the lime kiln in point 5*. Emerge by a signpost.

Follow the footpath **diagonally left** through the wooden 'gate' in the electric fence. Cross the stile in the corner of the field. Cross the lane. Cross the stile. Head **diagonally right** across the next two small grazing fields, each time crossing the stile in the corner.

Go through the small gate and walk **straight ahead**. Go through the gate and walk **straight ahead** through the farm buildings. Head **left** briefly and then **straight ahead** to follow the lane from the start of the walk into Small Dole, across the footbridge and field, back to your car.

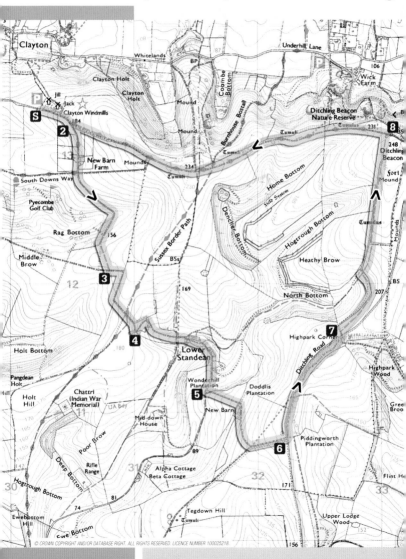

*Jack and Jill windmills*

A trek through open downland with gradients and views to lift the spirits and the chance to glimpse how farming and wildlife could co-exist to flourish in the South Downs.

**CREATIVE STARTING POINTS**

- Tradition versus innovation
- Wind and earth
- Water and food
- Romance, nostalgia, reality

**START** Entrance to car park by Jill windmill, Clayton.

**GRID REF** TQ 302 133

**TOTAL ASCENT** 795 ft/242 m

**PARKING** Car park at Jack and Jill windmills, Clayton.

**PUBLIC TRANSPORT**

*Train* station in Hassocks.

**TERRAIN** Downland walking on mud, grass or flint tracks. **Dogs strictly on short leads** through grazing fields, the pig farm and at Ditchling Beacon Nature Reserve.

**REFRESHMENTS** The Jack and Jill Inn in Clayton, *T* 01273 843595, or the various cafes and pubs in Hassocks.

**OS MAP** Explorer 122: Brighton and Hove

# 15 Windmills, Wildlife, Flint and Farming

*Jack and Jill Windmills Society (www.jillwindmill.org.uk) have done an excellent job in restoring and maintaining Jill Windmill. She has been restored to working order and now occasionally produces limited edition stoneground wholemeal flour, the vast majority of which is ground from local wheat and is on sale to visitors.*

*Jack, meanwhile, was once owned by Henry Longhurst, golf writer and commentator, who lived in the mill. Prior to that, Jack was home to writer and archaeologist, Edward Martin, for three years. Martin would go on to write 'Life in a Sussex Windmill', in which he portrays life in an old mill high on the downs.*

*The very earliest windmill on this site, then known as Duncton, first appeared on a map in 1780. No illustrations of this mill survive but it's believed that John Constable may have painted her during visits to Brighton in the 1820s.*

**S**  TQ 302 133 Turn **left** out of the car park (or take the small loop right after Jill windmill at the far end of the car park if you wish to see the windmills at close quarters). Walk up the stony bridleway.

**2**  TQ 304 132 At the fork, walk **right** along the South Downs Way towards Devil's Dyke.

Walk **straight on** through the farm buildings. At the 'crossroads' walk **straight on** towards the Chattri War Memorial. Walk with Poynings Golf Course on your right. Trek up the slope.

*Look out for hares around Pyecombe Golf Course and on the South Downs. Their main habitat is farmland but they can also be found on chalk downland and marshes. The distinctive silhouette of these magical animals is now significantly less common in many areas of Sussex. Why the decline? Hares graze different crops at different times of the year, moving from field to field in a seasonal pattern. Significant changes in farming in recent years – the decline of the rotational ley system, the reduction in biodiversity due to herbicide use and techniques such as straw burning (now banned) – have affected these seasonal patterns and have all helped contribute to the reduction in numbers.*

*At the same time, intensive farming practices have resulted in larger fields and less cover for hares and their main predator, the fox, has become more abundant. Leverets (young hares) are particularly vulnerable, relying on cover to remain safe. Each leveret holes up separately and their mother only visits once a day to reduce scent tracks and evade the powerful nose of the fox!*

**3** TQ 307 121 At the T-junction turn **left**, following the waymarked bridleway. Go through the gate, turning to follow the path **right**. Turn **left** to walk through the gate. As you pass the gates (and a crossroads of paths) further along the field boundary, walk **straight on** staying on this bridleway, which turns 90 degrees left before the next gate.

**4** TQ 310 116 At the next gate, follow the path **right** through the gate. **Dogs strictly on leads** through this grazing field, currently home to outdoor-bred pigs. Follow the bridleway. At the marker post walk **straight ahead**, following the blue arrow. Walk through South Down Flint Works and Standean Farm. Walk on past the buildings, up the slope.

*In the war, Standean Farm was used as a training camp. Standean is now a mixed farm with a local butcher's shop in Hassocks. The current family have run this extensive farm since 1932, adapting to survive through challenging times whilst also caring for the environment. Animals are kept outside wherever possible. You may see piles of compost as you walk through. This is garden waste which the farmer imports to avoid using artificial compost.*

*Look out for skylarks as Standean encourage them with 'skylark plots' – bare patches for skylarks in the midst of wheat fields, field margins left fallow to encourage diversity and wildlife and plots for nesting birds. Standean participates in the Higher Level Scheme of Conservation.*

*Path above Standean Farm.*

# 15 Windmills, Wildlife, Flint and Farming

5 **TQ 316 111** At the marker post, turn **left** along the footpath. Turn **right** at New Barn. Either go through the gate if open or across the stile and walk on. As you stroll up the track, look for the distant Chattri War Memorial on your right. *The Chattri is a moving war memorial to Hindu and Sikh soldiers who served in the First World War and died in hospital at Brighton.* Turn **left** to follow the grassy track up the hill. Cross the stile and Ditchling Road (fast cars!). Go through the gate opposite.

*View from ridge above Ditchling Beacon*

6  **TQ 322 108** Walk **left** towards High Park along the grassy ride. Keep **straight ahead** at the dew pond. See the Amex Stadium on your right. Walk through the gate. Follow the bridleway as it runs through the copse. The road runs parallel. At the marker post, turn **left**. Go back across Ditchling Road.

7  **TQ 326 116** Walk through the gate and follow the bridleway. Go through the next gate. Turn **right** and walk along the top of the field. Turn **left** in the corner. At the far corner, turn right, following the flinty, signed track up the hill. Go through the gate at the top and round the cattle pen. Walk **straight ahead** along the fence. Go through a gate. Keep walking north – **straight ahead** along the fence as the path opens into a field. *There are foot-stopping views to the North Downs over the Weald as you reach the ridge-top.*

8  **TQ 330 131** Go through the gate. *This is Ditchling Beacon, at 248m, the highest point in East Sussex. See the 'Downland Doddle' route for information about the SWT nature reserve here.* Turn **left** towards Keymer Post along the South Downs Way. Go through the gate. Pass an open pond on your left then restored dew pond Burnt House Pond. *Take a look at this classic downland feature, vital to help maintain wildlife diversity.*

   Go through another gate – Keymer Post which roughly marks the border between East and West Sussex. **Walk on.** Go through another gate. See Wolstonbury Hill ahead. Keep walking **straight ahead**. Jack beckons you home and then Jill.

*I once asked a downland farmer what conditions make it hardest to farm. 'Hot summers,' he answered, 'because all the water drains away.' Dew ponds are a way in which farmers traditionally collected rain to provide water for cows and sheep, by lining the bottom of the pond with clay to prevent rain water seeping away. Today, farmers may pipe water in or use troughs to store water but it's important that dew ponds are still maintained to help support the wide variety of wildlife such as dragonflies and greater-crested newts which rely upon this watery habitat to help them survive.*

*Agricultural downland between Ditchling Beacon and Falmer*

A surprisingly peaceful walk, given its proximity to Brighton. Judge for yourself whether the Amex Stadium *(see page 105)* successfully blends into the landscape as you meander through timeless downland towards Falmer. Return through agricultural fields to join the South Downs Way as it leads you back towards Ditchling Beacon. Before going home, have a little gander at Sussex Wildlife Trust's nature reserve beside the car park: it's often missed by Beacon visitors.

CREATIVE
STARTING POINTS

- Conflict versus harmony
- Circles
- Texture
- Man and beast

**START** Ditchling Beacon car park.
**GRID REF** TQ 333 130
**TOTAL ASCENT** 822 ft/250 m
**PARKING** Ditchling Beacon car park
£2 mobile phone parking. You have
until midnight to register/pay through
Ringco to the National Trust.
**TERRAIN** Easy to navigate once you
spot the first bridleway. Dogs strictly
on leads at Ditchling Beacon Nature
Reserve due to grazing sheep.

**REFRESHMENTS** Seasonal ice
cream van at Ditchling Beacon.
Optional extension to the cheap
and cheerful Swan Inn at Falmer,
*T* 01273 681 842, or the Half-Moon
at Plumpton, *T* 01273 890 253 with
its downland views.
**OS MAP** OS Explorer 122: Brighton
and Hove

The Amex Stadium is the American Express Community Stadium, home of Brighton and Hove Albion FC. The stadium is set three storeys down into the ground – 138,000 cubic metres of chalk were excavated for its construction! The structure of the stadium, designed by London-based architect, KSS, allows for a further tier to be added if expansion is needed. Local opinion on how well it blends into the landscape varies. Some support it whole-heartedly, others find it too prominent from a distance but believe it nestles into the landscape better as you approach. Others like the shape whilst some dislike the colour. Make up your own mind as you walk.

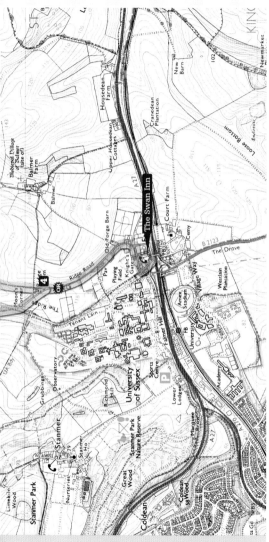

# 16 Downland Doddle with a Choice of Pubs

*Grazing at
Ditchling Beacon*
*The nature reserve at
Ditchling Beacon is owned
and managed by Sussex
Wildlife Trust. This includes
the plateau at the top where
the bridleway forms part
of the South Downs Way.
You may find traditional
breeds of sheep, such as
herdwick, grazing free
range. Such traditional
breeds are a very effective
conservation tool. Their
daily munch on nettles and
brambles helps controls the
spread of scrub, enabling
wildflowers such as horse-
shoe vetch and round-
headed rampion to grow
and encouraging increasing
biodiversity. Take a peek
and in season you may see
fragrant or common spotted
and twayblade orchids.
Look out for butterflies
such as the brown argus,
green hairstreak and then
common or chalkhill blue.
The easiest access is from
the bridleway (the South
Downs Way) which runs
along the plateau from
the car park. Paths within
the fenced reserve are too
dangerous for walking as
they are steep and slippery.*

**S** TQ 333 130 Head **east** across Ditchling Beacon road and go through the gate. Pass Ditchling Beacon dew pond to your right. Walk along the South Downs Way (SDW).

**2** TQ 338 128 Go **right** through a partially obscured, unsigned gate where the scrub alongside the path ends. (If you're having trouble spotting it and you reach the bridleway post pointing left on the SDW you've gone too far!) Follow the track diagonally across the field. Go through the next gate, marked with a blue arrow, into the grazing field. Walk **straight ahead** to follow the track into the trees. Soon the path runs along a fence. Ignore the gate with the marker post at the path junction. Walk **straight ahead** with the fence on your right. See the Amex Stadium ahead. Go through the gate and follow the fenced path down towards the house. Pass through the pens.

**3** TQ 347 108 Walk **straight ahead** along the track, passing St Mary's Farmhouse on your left. See the new University of Sussex (my old stomping ground) accommodation blocks on your right. Further along, glimpse Brighton to your right and the Amex Stadium as you follow the lane into Falmer.

**4** TQ 350 098 At the lay-by, you have a choice:

**OPTIONAL ROUTE** For the Swan Inn, a free house with good cheap pub food: follow the lane 1.2km into Falmer. Turn **left** at Mill Street then **right** down Park Street to visit the Swan Inn. Altogether, this pub loop adds around 1.5km to your walk.

*Sussex Wildlife Trust sheep*

**MAIN ROUTE** You may prefer not to continue to Falmer but to stay on our main loop. Look for the wooden way-marked bridleway. Turn **left**, almost doubling-back upon yourself. Walk along the narrow stony path. Pass a ruined flint farm cottage. Continue walking. **Pass and ignore** a gate where a bridleway forks left. Stay on your path hence keeping to the 'totty' land, and giving yourself some beautiful views over Faulkner's Bottom to the left. Go through the gate and keep walking. **Continue** to the next gate and keep onwards to join the wide chalk and flint South Downs Way. Keep walking **straight ahead**. Go through yet another gate and along the narrow path.

5 **TQ 370 125** Arrive at the crossroads. Turn **left** and follow the flinty and now signed SDW 4km back to Ditchling Beacon. Thirsty and hungry folks should look out for the bridleway leading right down steep 'Plumpton Bostall' to the Half-Moon pub.

*Sussex Dialect*
*'Totty' land is a Sussex phrase for high land and like much Sussex dialect, it's derived from an Anglo-Saxon word – in this case, 'totian', meaning to elevate. Other Sussex dialect words are 'rife', meaning small river – particularly across the West Sussex coastal plain; 'fret', meaning sea-fog; 'laines', meaning open tracts of land at the base of the Downs and 'knap', 'knep' or 'kneb', meaning small hill. Look out for place names derived from Sussex dialect such as Knepp Castle, Ferring Rife and the North Laine in Brighton.*

*Downland flowers at Blackcap*

# Sussex Walks

## The South Downs
## – West of Brighton

This is a very satisfying area to walk. Good stretches of downland track combine with broadleaf woodland and scrubby copses, with settlements and distant views over the Chichester Estuary to make your experience interesting and enjoyable.

There are a number of historic elements to look out for: our Lavant walk *(see page 110)* explores a possible link with Blake, the walk from Bignor Hill *(see page 122)* follows a Roman road along a hilltop before descending to explore the downland village of Slindon and don't forget Cissbury! Cissbury Ring *(see page 133)* is one of those places that's sometimes missed because it's just 'there', in relatively close proximity to Worthing. It is however, a very interesting place, significant in terms of both history and ecology. I'll tell you something else about it too: it may be right under our noses but has a true downland feel to it.

Away from the Downs, our coastal trail encourages you to take a closer look at the sea. The Tidal Creek and East Head walk *(see page 130)* enables you to explore this unique, evolving location.

*Path near Stump Bottom*

*Sheep on downland*

This walk has everything! It's easy to navigate, has a bit of climbing to keep you fit and offers beautiful views over downland to Chichester Estuary. There's even a choice of two noteworthy pubs and some local gossip about the poet William Blake. Was he inspired to write certain stanzas in Jerusalem hereabouts?

## CREATIVE STARTING POINTS

- Diagonals
- Feast or famine
- Shades of green and white
- Up, down and all around

**START** At the bottom of the concrete steps opposite The Triangle car park.
**GRID REF** SU 879 113
**TOTAL ASCENT** 746 ft/227 m
**PARKING** Travelling south from Singleton: leave the A286 to drive south along Town Lane. Turn left for the Triangle car park or keep straight ahead for alternative parking at Seven Points.

**PUBLIC TRANSPORT**
*Train* Fishbourne Station (4km – accessed via Centurion's Way).
**TERRAIN** Flinty bridleway or grassy downland paths with some climbing. Easy to navigate.
**REFRESHMENTS**
The Earl of March, *T* 01243 533 993; The Royal Oak, *T* 01243 527 434, both in or near East Lavant.
**OS MAP** Explorer 120: Chichester

# 17 A Walk through Green and Pleasant Lan>

**S** SU 879 113 Walk up the steps and turn **right**, following the footpath through the gate. Continue up the hill. *Views over racecourse to left and back over Weald and Downland.* Towards the top, veer **right** (currently mesh fencing around masts runs alongside path.) Visit the trig point to left – the panoramic 360-degree views are worth a few steps! Return to your grassy track and **walk south-west**. The path becomes flinty. Go through the gate and follow the track to the Seven Points car park.

**2** SU 871 109 At Seven Points car park, turn **left** towards Lavant. Walk along the flinty path. *Chalkpit Lane may be uneven underfoot but is fairly easy walking, heading downhill with occasional Land Rovers! You are heading towards Chichester Cathedral.* The path flattens out as you approach East Lavant.

**SU 865 086** Turn **right** at the road and walk through East Lavant. Pass or go into The Royal Oak Freehouse and Restaurant. *(Given 5\* in the Michelin guide, it's highly tempting!)* Pass the church. When the road forks, walk **diagonally right** along Sheepwash Lane. *Look out for the startlingly clear waters of the River Lavant.*

**SU 860 083** At the bridleway signpost by the bridge: OPTIONAL ROUTE: To walk 150m to the Earl of March pub, walk **straight ahead** for a short distance (50m). At the sign-post, turn **left** into the recreation ground to follow the footpath as it heads **right**. Walk up the slight slope to the pub.

*Chalkpit Lane*

# 17 A Walk through Green and Pleasant Land

*In William Blake's footsteps?*
*The poet, engraver and artist*
*William Blake, spent three*
*years living in Felpham.*
*Escaping a breadline*
*existence and ill health,*
*he left London to accept*
*his friend William Hayley's*
*invitation to recuperate*
*in Sussex. In return, he*
*illustrated Hayley's*
*writing. There's little*
*evidence to show that*
*Blake's time in Sussex*
*influenced his work but,*
*since this was Blake's only*
*stay in the countryside,*
*it is perfectly possible that*
*the familiar words of*
*'Jerusalem' – now known to*
*many as a hymn – were the*
*'fruits of quiet vigils in*
*neighbouring woods.'*

*'And did these feet*
*in ancient time.*
*Walk upon England's*
*mountains green?*
*And was the holy*
*Lamb of God*
*On England's*
*pleasant pastures seen?'*

*In 1804, Blake was tried*
*and acquitted in Chichester*
*for 'sedition and treasonable*
*speech' after a scuffle with*
*a drunken soldier in Felpham.*
*Shortly after this, he left*
*Sussex. I have sited*
*this route thereabouts so*
*that you may walk in*
*Blake's footsteps.*
*Perhaps you'll even be*
*moved to creativity...*

**MAIN ROUTE** Turn **right** across the bridge towards Staple House Farm. Walk **straight ahead**. This flat grassy path continues for some time. Do not cross the small river which runs alongside the path. Pass through the gate into West Dean Estate and walk **straight ahead**. Stay on this path. (The Centurion Cycleway runs parallel with this path, about 75m to the west.) Walk through the gateway.

5 SU 856 106 At the four-way wooden waymarker, turn **diagonally right** to walk north-east up the steep downland slope. Go through the gate and continue on the narrow path. See the masts ahead. *Enjoy far-reaching views over a rolling landscape of downland pasture, Chichester cathedral, the sea and tidal estuary.* At the top, pass the double-fronted flint 'Rubbing House'. Walk **straight ahead** at the signpost.

**6** **SU 871 109** You are back at Seven Points car park. To continue to the Triangle car park, walk past the seven-point signpost. Follow the footpath towards the Trundle. At the gates, go through the **right-hand** gate following the blue arrow for the bridleway. Walk **straight ahead**. Stay roughly parallel with the fence (about 30m at most) along the grassy mud track. Go through the gate at the end. Follow the signed footpath **left** through the trees. Stay on this path until you emerge opposite the racecourse on the road. Turn **left** for a short stretch along the busy road back to the Triangle car park.

*Blake is believed to have stayed upstairs at the Earl of March where he may have gazed out at the scene beyond the bakehouse and stables. Did words and phrases leap into his mind whilst he was in Lavant, inspired by the view towards the Downs? Was his work influenced by his time Mid-Lavant, where William used to visit his friend, Miss Poole, thought by some to be his muse?*

*Or perhaps, as The Rev J.H. Bodgener points out in Sussex County Magazine in 1954, Blake was 'never infatuated with external nature'. He quotes Blake's declaration that 'I paint through the eye, not with the eye … perfectly from vision, others imperfectly from nature'.*

*Blake's window?*

# 18 A Downland Meander to Cissbury Ring

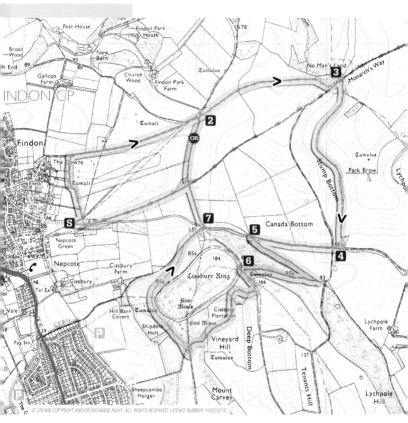

A pleasant walk through agricultural downland offering lovely views and a feeling of open space and wildness culminating in the chance to explore or relax at the historic site of Cissbury Ring.

10.8 km / 6.75 miles

- High and low
- Distant or close
- Important versus insignificant, seen and unseen
- Illumination and shadows

Cissbury Ring

**START** The gate and bridleway sign behind the lay-by opposite Nepcote Green Recreation Ground.

**GRID REF** TQ 129 085

**TOTAL ASCENT** 923 ft/281 m

**PARKING** Nepcote Green Recreation Ground, via Nepcote Lane off Findon Road (A24). From Nepcote Lane in Findon, follow the blue pedestrian sign for Cissbury Ring. Don't go as far as the parking area at Cissbury but stop at the large lay-by opposite the grassy recreation ground at Nepcote Green. *Note: Not to be confused with Cissbury* *car park at Storrington Rise in Findon Valley.*

**PUBLIC TRANSPORT**

*Bus* see *www.stagecoachbus.com*

**TERRAIN** Good clear paths, with one or two steepish climbs.

**REFRESHMENTS** Findon is a picturesque flint village. Try the Gun Inn (Observer food Awards, dog-friendly in bar), *T* 01903 873 206, or the Village House Coaching Inn, *T* 01903 873 350.

**OS MAP** Explorer 121: Arundel and Pulborough

*Look out for the 'Wattle House' on Nepcote Green – the current brick and flint building is believed to have replaced an original smaller ramshackle 'wattle' store. These wattles were panels of lightweight fencing created by weaving thin branches between sturdier uprights. Nepcote Green was the site of many a sheep fair and the building was used to store the wattles for sheep pens. See www.findonvillage.com*

*Findon has a history of links with horse racing and today there is still a racing stable here. The gallops are still used to train racehorses and Grand National winners such as Aldaniti (1981) and Jerry M (1912) have trained here.*

**TQ 129 085** Walk to the metal gate behind the car park. Walk **left** at the four way marker post along the byway. Bear **right** by the marker post at the fork, continuing to walk alongside the Gallops.

Turn **right** at the T-junction with the chalk track and walk up the byway, signed with a green arrow on the marker post. *See the ramparts of Cissbury on your right and the sea beyond Worthing.*

Pass a bridleway gate and keep walking **straight ahead**. After some distance, pass another small bridleway gate just before the fenced field running alongside you ends.

**TQ 139 094** At the crossroads marker post, continue **straight ahead** along the mud byway but **be careful** – you need to **take the right hand track** so that fence will be on your left.

**OPTIONAL ROUTE** For a short cut direct to Cissbury Ring, head **right** along the bridleway.

**MAIN ROUTE** Walk **up and along** this mud track through agricultural downland for some time. *Glimpse the sea and Cissbury on your right.* Take care when you start to go downhill, keep **left** at the fork. Continue on down into No Man's Land. *This scrubby copse is a peaceful, wild spot with occasional buzzards circling.* Keep **right** at the marker post taking the less obvious track which descends fairly steeply. Pass across Monarch's Way. Stay on your bridleway, following the blue arrow until it ends abruptly at a field.

**TQ 151 097** Walk **right** through the small gate and along the narrow fenced track which wends its way along Stump Bottom. There are grazing fields on both sides beyond fences. At the end of the track, pass restored Lychpole Dewpond.

**TQ 151 183** Turn **right**, passing through the gateway and along the byway. Pass the green barn.

*Walking on the ramparts*

*The ancient monument of Cissbury Ring is set high on a chalk promontory. The name is thought to come from Cissa, Son of Ælla, Saxon Invader and Burh, meaning stronghold and today, it's still possible to see what a powerful location this is. Cissbury has played many important roles in history. The large craters on the western side are the remains of Neolithic workings when shafts of up to 12m deep were cut into the chalk to excavate flint in this important mining area. The ramparts are evidence of its later use as an Iron Age hill fort, a part of Roman defences against the Saxons. More recently, in WW2, it was fortified with gun emplacements. Now owned by the National Trust, its significance today is more in terms of the unique habitat it offers after centuries of continuous grazing.*

*The site has been given the status of Site of Special Scientific Interest due to its nationally rare unimproved chalk grassland. Look out for plants such as round-headed rampion, also known as 'the pride of Sussex' and orchids. Some of the plants here are significant because of the food which they provide for butterflies, including rarities such as the adonis blue (See the Wolstonbury route for more information on the adonis blue).*

5 **TQ 143 083** Turn **left** through the gate onto the National Trust land at Cissbury Ring after about 100m. Follow the track for about 800m until the next NT sign. **Do not** go straight ahead through the gate but stay on NT land, **doubling back right** and up the hill. *The narrow and sometimes steep path is bordered by thicket and scrub.* At the top, pass the marker post and head **straight on**.

6 **TQ 142 081** At the second marker post, see the gate and Cissbury Ring ahead. I suggest that the best way to soak up the atmosphere and history of this rugged but beautiful spot is to walk around the ramparts. You may also follow the bridleway which circles the exterior of the fort. To reach it, turn **left** at the post and then **right** to follow track around the fort.

The ramparts or bridleway will lead you round to the north/north-west side of the fort. A narrow chalky track leads through the ramparts to the bridleway and you may see a small parking area below. Walk **along** and then **left** down the wood-edged steps.

Go through the kissing gate and continue on to National Trust information board. Leave Cissbury Ring.

7 **TQ 139 084** Follow the signed bridleway **straight ahead** past the parking area. Turn **left** at the marker post/end of field to join the Monarch's Way. Walk along this narrow fenced track. Turn **right** at the lane to rejoin your car.

*Cissbury Ring*

# 19 **A Walk Through Time and Traditions**

Stane Street

Begin with an empowering hilltop stretch along the Roman road Stane Street, which leads you onwards through ever-changing broadleaf woodland. Descend past the folly to the flint village of Slindon, where seasonal displays may be on display in Autumn. The steady climb back up to Bignor Hill is strangely satisfying with an ever-increasing feeling of space and scale.

### 13.5 km / 8.4 miles

- Seasonal, constant
- Hub versus space
- Along and through
- Animal, vegetable, mineral

**START** At the large signpost in Bignor Hill car park.

**GRID REF** SU 972 129

**TOTAL ASCENT** 976 ft/297 m

**PARKING** Bignor Hill National Trust car park. *Note: unmade road on approach from Bignor.*

**PUBLIC TRANSPORT**

*Bus* Regular *Compass* bus service 84-5, Worthing to Chichester, stopping at Fontwell village. Take London Road opposite bus stop, then bear left for the underpass beneath A27. This brings you out on Dukes Road, adjacent to Slindon South Lodge.

**TERRAIN** Chalk paths may be very slippery when wet.

**REFRESHMENTS** The Forge Community Cafe and shop in Slindon, at bottom of School Hill, *T* 01243 814 324. *Note: the pub marked on OS map is no more.*

**OS MAP** Explorer 121: Arundel and Pulborough

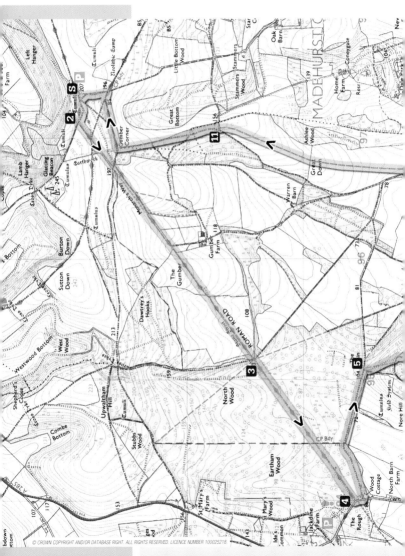

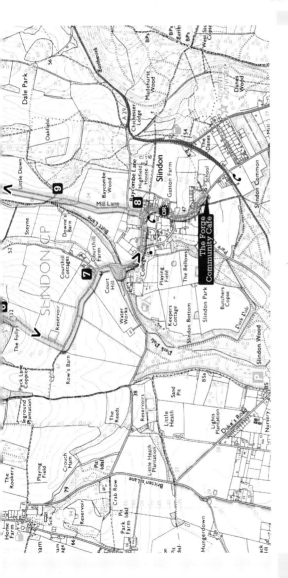

# 19 **A Walk Through Time and Traditions**

**SU 972 129** Follow the gravel track past the *No Cars* signpost. There's a second signpost behind the bush. Follow the South Downs Way towards Winchester. Stay on the gravel track for a shortish distance (**ignoring** grass track on the left) until the next wooden signpost. Turn **left** along the South Downs briefly. Walk down a tiny slope where the path hits a crossroads/signpost.

*This is Stane Street – part of the impressive Roman road which once ran between London and Chichester, helping the Roman military machine move efficiently. Today, Stane Street still leaves a strong impression on the Sussex landscape and this hilltop section is not to be missed.*

**SU 971 129** Turn **right** and then immediately **left**, leaving the South Downs Way to join the bridleway signed *To Gumber Bothy*.

At the stile and signpost, go **straight ahead** for Gumber Bothy. *Enjoy views straight ahead towards Chichester along the course of Stane Street and left towards the sea*. Various paths join. **Stay on Stane Street, walking straight ahead.** Reach a gate.

OPTIONAL ROUTE left to Gumber Bothy, a converted traditional Sussex barn where, the National Trust provide simple overnight accommodation or camping.

MAIN ROUTE Continue **straight ahead** through the gate. Walk on and at the next gate, go **straight ahead** on the narrow path beside the fence. Stane Street (and Monarch's Way) leads you through an atmospheric broadleaf wood, where wind rustles through the leaves.

**SU 951 114** Reach a lovely spot with a bench and six-way signpost. Walk **straight ahead** towards Halnaker. Continue on this path, over a cross bridleway until you reach a wide gravel bridleway at a curve. Turn **left** for 50m to a road.

### 13.5 km / 8.4 miles

**SU 939 105** Turn **left** to walk 25m along the roadside. Turn **left** along the signed public bridleway through North Wood. Walk past the huts and onwards. At the fork, go **right** past the marker post with the blue bridleway arrow. At the next fork, again go **right** past the marker post with the blue bridleway arrow. This is an uphill stretch!

**SU 950 104** At the marker post/crossroads, turn **right** along the bridleway and up the slope. At the top of the slope, by the right hand marker post, walk **straight on**. At the next marker post, fork **left** along the ride, following the footpath/National Trust *Fancy a swift one?* marker. Veer **left** at the fork. *Look out for bluebells in season.*

**SU 956 097** Reach the gate/edge of the woods. Views open out over forest, fields and downs. Turn **right** along the footpath. You will soon reach Slindon Folly (a.k.a. Nore Folly) and trig point.

Follow the gravel path down. Turn **left** at the farm track.

*Don't miss Slindon or 'Nore' Folly – an early 19th century listed flint structure! This 'eye-catcher' appears to serve no real purpose. There was once a room behind it where shooting parties ate luncheon. Now, it resembles a tunnel but through what? Time? Or does it simply serve to frame a snapshot of the world? There's a bench for picnics.*

*View from Great Down of grazing sheep on downland*

# 19 **A Walk Through Time and Traditions**

*Slindon is a picturesque flint village. In October, look out for a colourful display of the year's harvest at Slindon Pumpkins. You may wish to browse Slindon Pottery. And look out for Bleak House, the first family home of Hilaire Belloc and his wife Elodie. Hilaire Belloc grew up in Slindon and was a true Sussex man. He was particularly fond of the Western South Downs and wrote several books about Sussex including 'Ha'nacker Mill', 'The South Country', 'Sussex' and 'The County of Sussex'. Many people know him for his work 'The Four Men: A Farrago', in which four characters, each aspects of his personality, travel the width of Sussex from Robertsbridge to Harting.*

**7** **SU 959 087** At Court Hill Farm building, turn **right** along the road. Look out for the narrow cutting which runs to the **left** of the road and which leads you to the village. At the road, turn left towards Slindon. Pass Slindon College and St Richard's Church and stay on the Top Road.

**8** **SU 964 084**

**OPTIONAL ROUTE** For the Forge Community Cafe and shop, follow the lane down School Hill. The road curves round and the planned cafe is sited in the old forge: please check the website **www.slindonforge.co.uk**

**MAIN ROUTE** To continue on the main walk, turn **left** up Mill Lane. Leave the road towards the top of the hill where it curves to walk **straight ahead** around the gate. Follow the bridleway through the National Trust Slindon Estate. *This fenced path gives views over the ridge where Stane Street is.* At the first fork (unsigned), keep straight on the tree-lined path. At the signpost, **take the right fork** along the bridleway.

**9** **SU 965 091** Soon there's another signed junction: walk **straight ahead** across the fields on the bridleway to Bignor. There's a low hedge and a barbed wire fence on your left.

**10** **SU 967 101** At the signpost, walk **straight ahead** between the fields. This is a long gradual climb through chalky fields. Go through the gate and walk **straight on** through the grazing field. Continue on your steady upward path.

**SU 970 117** At the end of the field, go through the gate and walk **straight ahead** into the woods. At the first marker post, keep walking **straight ahead**. At the second marker post, walk **straight ahead** again. The track follows the edge of the woods. Keep walking **straight ahead** at the next marker post, still climbing slowly upwards. At the signpost, turn **right** along the flinty path that lies between field and woods. *Far-reaching views towards the sea.* At the next two signposts to offshoot paths, keep walking **straight ahead**. At the junction at the end, turn **left** up the slope to the car park.

*Stane Street*

# 20 The Tidal Creek and West Wittering

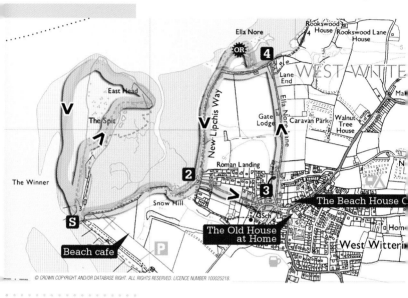

© CROWN COPYRIGHT AND/OR DATABASE RIGHT. ALL RIGHTS RESERVED. LICENCE NUMBER 100025218.

The Manhood Peninsula, with its beautiful light and atmospheric landscape, is a favourite location of many artists, photographers and sea-side lovers.

Find out why on this stroll around West Wittering and the evolving nature reserve of East Head. This mile-long sand spit joins the mainland at the 'Hinge' and so far, is withstanding the forces of the sea. Enjoy sea air, beach life and some interesting wildlife habitats. This is more than just a beach.

5 km / 2.8 miles or East Head Sand Spit loop 2.6 km / 1.6 miles

*Tidal Creek and East Head Shingle Spit*

CREATIVE
STARTING POINTS

- Ebb and flow
- Texture and rhythm
- Temperature, tone, silhouettes
- Evolving versus disappearing
- Peace, movement, noise

**START** At the far end of the car park, by the end of the tarmac road.

**GRID REF** SZ 765 984

**TOTAL ASCENT** 27 ft/8 m (almost downhill!)

**PARKING** (with WC) Large grassy car park at West Wittering. See *www.westwitteringbeach.co.uk*

**PUBLIC TRANSPORT**

*Bus* Nearest bus stop in the village. Timetable at *www.stagecoachbus. com/south*. More bus information at *www.conservancy.co.uk*

**TERRAIN** Easy, flat walking on mainly hard surfaces. The extra loop around the spit is sandy underfoot and may be wet.

**REFRESHMENTS** Beach cafe and takeaway can be very busy in high season. Try in West Wittering village: Beach House Cafe, (picnic hampers to go), *T* 01243 514 800; or The Old House at Home, (pub with large garden), *T* 01243 572 477.

**OS MAP** Explorer 120: Chichester

# 20 The Tidal Creek and West Wittering

*See Snow Hill Marsh on your right and tidal waters to the left. Pass the crabbing pool on the edge of the marsh where you may crab at high tide. Snow Hill Marsh is managed by West Wittering estate and is a salt marsh. Plants to look out for include: sea purslane, rice grass, eel grass, glasswort, sea lavender, sea blight, sea aster, sea purslane, saltmarsh grass.*

**1** **SZ 765 984** Just before the mini-roundabout, turn **right** to walk along the firebreak and join the path which leads along the shoreline. Walk along the path **away** from the flagpole and East Head spit opposite. Pass a bench.

**2** **SZ 773 986** Go **right** at the four-way wooden way-marker, through the gate and along the tarmacked public footpath through Roman Landing Estate. Follow the public footpath **straight ahead** through the gate. Walk along the narrow, fenced track through the grazing fields. At the end, turn **right** to go onto the road. *The Church of St Peter is to your right.* Turn **left** along the road. *West Wittering village is further along this road.*

**3** **SZ 778 985** Turn **left** along Ellanore Lane to follow the signed, public footpath. Follow this hard-surfaced path for some way. At the end, you will see the sea once more!

*Tidal Creek*

5 km / 2.8 miles or East Head Sand Spit loop 2.6 km / 1.6 miles

**SZ 778 994** Turn **left** at the wooden waymarker. Go through the gate onto Chichester Harbour Conservancy Land. Walk along this sheltered, hedged and hard-surfaced path.

OPTIONAL ROUTE At the wooden waymarker, go **right**, leaving the upper track to follow a small diversion around Ella Nore head-land. Tidal pools may straddle the path making water-proof shoes a must. Rejoin the upper footpath and turn right.

MAIN ROUTE Pass the bench and disused old bird hide. Turn **left**, following the public or permissive footpath. See the spit across the tidal creek. The path wends its way back through the scrub along the coastline to emerge at the familiar village green (**point S**). Turn **right** across the green, returning to the beach along the earlier footpath.

Continued on next page...

# 20 The Tidal Creek and West Wittering

*Plants to look out for on the dunes include marram grass, common gorse, red fescue, ragwort, slack glasswort, sea purslane, tree lupin, seaclub rush, yellow horned poppy, sea beet, sea holly, sand couch, lyme grass.*

**Marram grass**

*This tough plant plays a vital role in preserving the landscape, trapping sand and binding the dunes together with its long roots. It grows through new sand to avoid being buried. Please do not walk on the grass as being trampled by human feet can kill it. Without the marram grass, the dunes will disappear on the sea breeze.*

*Birds which you may spot during your walk in the appropriate season include:*
**Waders:** *curlew, whimbrel, godwit, oystercatcher, redshank, turnstone, dunlin, sanderling, lapwing, ringed plover, grey plover, golden plover, greenshank, sandpiper*
**Geese:** *brent geese*
**Ducks:** *shelduck, mallard, wigeon, teal, redbreasted merganser*
**Herons:** *grey heron, little egret*
**Terns:** *sandwich tern, common tern, little cormorant.*

**Don't miss the opportunity to explore East Head Sand Spit whilst you're here!**

Back by the start, turn **right** at the flag. Walk past the information board and follow the path along the fence. Where the path forks, head **right** between the roped-off sand dunes and walk along the water's edge. At the dog bins, go **left**, up the boardwalk. It's possible to follow this boardwalk to the very end of East Head. The sand dunes are more extensive than you might imagine and well worth taking the time to explore but do stay on the boardwalks to help this fragile environment continue to flourish.

East Head is a National Trust reserve which consists of a natural, constantly-evolving sand and shingle spit. It has a very special, remote feel with sea breezes, sailing boats and unusual plants. Since 1966, when the National Trust acquired the land, this vibrant and dynamic environment has doubled in size. We may think of conserving nature as protecting it from change but sometimes allowing somewhere the time and space to develop is equally important.

East Head is a Site of Special Scientific Interest. It's also a designated Ramsar Site because of its significance for coastal birds. There are many different habitats packed into this small area including sand dunes, salt marsh, wetlands and reedbeds.

Marram grass

# About the Author

## THE AUTHOR

**Deirdre Huston** is an outdoor photographer and guide-book author with an interest in history and ecology. She makes short films mixing archive materials with contemporary research. Author of *Day Walks on the South Downs* and *Cycling Days Out – South East England*, her work is frequently inspired by the outdoors. Deirdre is a member of the Outdoor Writers and Photographers Guild. See *www.deirdrehuston.co.uk* for further information.

Deirdre is a qualified teacher and part-time lecturer in photography. She lives with her husband and three children in Sussex.

## VERTEBRATE PUBLISHING

**Vertebrate Publishing** is an independent publisher dedicated to producing the very best outdoor leisure titles. We have critically acclaimed and award-winning titles covering a range of leisure activities, including; mountain biking, cycling, rock climbing, hill walking and others. We are best known for our titles such as *Lake District Mountain Biking*, and *Revelations* – the autobiography of British rock climber Jerry Moffatt, awarded the Grand Prize at the 2009 Banff Mountain Book Festival.

For more information about Vertebrate Publishing please visit our website: *www.v-publishing.co.uk*

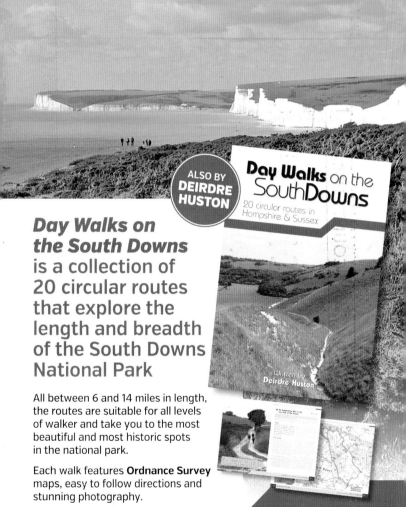